TAKING A STAND AGAINST SEXISM AND SEX DISCRIMINATION

TAKING A STAND AGAINST SEXISM AND SEX DISCRIMINATION

BY TRUDY J. HANMER

Franklin Watts 1990
New York London Toronto Sydney

Photographs courtesy of: Photo Researchers: pp. 13 (Joseph Szabo), 94 (Bettye Lane), 102 (Jan Lukes), 105 (Ursula Markus); Randy Matusow: pp. 14, 113; The Bettmann Archive: pp. 21, 31, 46, 60, 66, 73, 79, 88, 93; UPI/Bettmann Newsphotos: pp. 26, 72, 80, 91, 98, 99; National Park Service, Womens Rights Historical Park: p. 57; Brown Brothers: p. 63; Bettye Lane: pp. 97, 109, 120, 131; Jeff Greenberg: p. 108

Library of Congress Cataloging-in-Publication Data

Hanmer, Trudy J.
Taking a stand against sexism and sex discrimination / by Trudy J. Hanmer.
p.   cm.
Includes bibliographical references and index.
Summary: Discusses the origins of unequal treatment of women, the history of the women's rights movement, and current issues facing women in the home, the workplace, and the justice system.
ISBN 0-531-10962-3
1. Feminism—United States—Juvenile literature. 2. Sex discrimination against women—United States—Juvenile literature. 3. Sexism—United States—Juvenile literature. 4. Women's rights—United States—Juvenile literature. [1. Feminism. 2. Sex discrimination against women. 3. Sexism. 4. Women's rights.]
I. Title.
HQ1426.H275   1990
305.42'0973—dc20   90-12567
CIP
AC

CONTENTS

For Fantasia

═══════ONE═══════

SEXISM AND SEX DISCRIMINATION:
WHO CARES?

The new father bursts into the hospital lounge
where the grandparents of the baby are anxiously
waiting. Joyously he shouts, "It's a boy!" Every
minute this scene is reenacted 7 times in the United
States and 266 times around the world. Whether
the delivery takes place in a modern hospital facil-
ity or in a simple home in a peasant village, the first
information given to the community about any infant is its sex. The baby's health, size, weight, eye
and hair color are usually reported shortly there-
after, but throughout the world a baby's sex is the
first and most important piece of information.

"It's a girl" or "It's a boy" are phrases that will
determine the course of the baby's life through
childhood to adulthood. How a person dresses,
acts, earns a living, fills leisure time, and relates to
children are all determined by sex, no matter what
society he or she enters. And, sadly, if the baby is a
girl born in the United States and most other coun-

tries, she can expect that many of the choices she faces in life will be limited by her sex, especially by other people's perceptions of how women should act and what women should do.

Assigning people specific roles in society based on gender is called sexism. Preventing people from holding certain jobs or establishing different laws for different people solely on the basis of sex is called sex discrimination. Sexism and sex discrimination are both present in American society today, although neither is as blatant as it once was. More and more people have come to believe that individuals should be allowed to choose their own roles and jobs, regardless of sex, and that in a democracy like the United States freedom should mean freedom from sex discrimination.

At the same time, there are other people who believe that the physical differences between women and men—especially the fact that women are the only people who can bear children—mean that the sexes must always be unequal. They also believe that laws that treat men and women differently are necessary for the protection of women and children. These people argue that sex discrimination is natural, that is, it is rooted in nature. They point to examples in the animal kingdom to support their argument. For example, they suggest that in many animal families it is the male who has a job outside his home—that of hunter, food gatherer, or protector—while the female has the job inside the home of bearing and raising the children.

Although human beings share a great deal with other mammals, over the course of American history Americans have come to question the wisdom of patterning human lives in a modern industrial society on the lives of animals living in the wild. At the time of the writing of the U.S. Constitution, the phrases "all men" or "all citizens" were generally accepted as meaning all white males in the country. Over the course of time these phrases have been broadened legally to include, first, all men, regardless of race. During the second half of the twentieth century "all men" under the law has increasingly come to mean "all people," regardless of sex.

In spite of this progress, however, sexism and sex discrimination continue to pervade American society. People who believe that men and women, girls and boys, in America have equal opportunities must consider the following:

- Recent studies show that teachers call on boys in classrooms from three to eight times more frequently than they call on girls.
- Women in America earn 63 cents for every dollar earned by men.
- Women's athletic budgets at schools and colleges average less than 20 percent of men's.
- One-third of the families headed by women live below the poverty line.
- By the twenty-first century 99 percent of the people on welfare will be women and dependent children.
- Of the brighter high school graduates who do *not* go on to college, 70 percent to 90 percent are girls.
- The life expectancy for American men is eight years shorter than that for women.

- As more men have entered the field of elementary education in the past twenty-five years, the pay scale in that profession has risen.
- As more women have entered the field of accounting in the past twenty-five years, the pay scale in that profession has remained static.
- In 1989, 62 percent of working women polled by the *New York Times* agreed with this statement: "Most men are willing to let women get ahead, but only if women do all the housework at home."[1]

All of these facts reveal the continuation of sexism and sex discrimination. Sexism influences the jobs open to women, the amount they are paid, and their opportunities for higher education. This, in turn, determines the power or lack of power that women have in society. Social ills such as pornography, date rape, and the battering of women are directly connected to women's lack of status and power.

Nor are men immune to problems caused by sexism. Men's shorter life expectancy and tendency to suffer more than women from a variety of stress-related diseases is also connected to sexism. Societal expectations that men be invariably strong, resilient, and the major financial support of their families often lead to unrealistic expectations for individual men, who ruin their health trying to live up to external expectations for their lives.

During the 1960s and 1970s the women's movement in the United States and throughout the world brought issues of sexism and sex discrimination to the forefront of people's consciousness.

Sex discrimination takes many forms.
At schools and colleges, athletic budgets
for women's sports such as field hockey
and volleyball average less than 20 percent
that allocated for men's sports.

*As more men have entered the field
of education in the past twenty-five years,
the pay scale has risen.*

Many people believe that the women's movement is no longer needed and that the job of eradicating sex discrimination has been completed. Unfortunately, there is still much to be done.

By tracing the history of sexism in the United States we can better understand what problems still remain. By understanding those problems we can develop strategies for taking a stand against sex discrimination, whether it is in the classroom, on the job, in laws, or in our homes. We must all care when any group of people is prevented from reaching their full potential because of ignorance and prejudice.

TWO

SEXISM AS A CONCEPT: IT ALL STARTED WITH ADAM AND EVE

The idea that men and women should play different roles in society is an ancient concept. Although Americans formed a new nation only a few hundred years ago, the majority of the peoples who came to this continent came from Europe or the British Isles. They shared a Judaic and Christian heritage in which roles for men and women were intricately interwoven with religious beliefs and daily customs. As new groups have come to America from Asia and from Central and South America, they have brought with them similar concepts of the role that gender must play in society. In general, men are assigned public roles, and women are assigned private roles. Men work outside the home, and women work within the home. The idea that women must take a predominantly domestic place in the world is a long-standing tradition.

Most of the world's religions stress different roles for men and women. In the Old Testament

Book of Genesis the story of Adam and Eve is presented as explaining the beginnings of life on earth. In this story Eve, the first woman on earth, is created as a helper for Adam. She is tempted by a serpent to defy God by eating fruit from the forbidden Tree of Knowledge. The consequences of her actions are severe: God tells her, first, that from this point on women will bear children in pain, and second, that her husband shall rule over her. This creation story is central to Christian and Judaic beliefs.

For hundreds of centuries custom and law have evolved from the roles assigned to men and women by this story, especially the customs and legal heritage shared by most Americans. From the reality of childbirth—that is, that only women have the capacity to bear children—has come the biological justification for sex discrimination. From the edict from God has come the justification for a hierarchy in which husband rules over wife and man rules over woman. In Western thought the natural progression is this: God, man, and, finally, woman.

BIOLOGICAL ARGUMENTS

The biological arguments underpinning sex discrimination have been perhaps the most compelling. Women alone give birth, and there are many reasons why mothers remain physically close to babies. The biological rationale for woman's subordinate position in society rests heavily on the assumption that biology is the same as nature and that there is a natural order of the universe that should not be upset. Because nature has ordained that women bear children, nature has logically ordained that women be softer, more caring, and more nurturing than men. Furthermore, biology and nature, because of childbearing and child rearing (especially nursing) restrict women's mobility. These restrictions have led to the creation of different spheres for men and women. Women, according to this argument, belong in the home, and men belong in the outside world.

Using biological arguments to explain human nature for either men or women reinforces the idea that the two sexes have relative positions of power. Anyone who speaks of women's nature or men's nature in the conventional sense is able to justify men's aggressiveness and domination and women's passivity. Behaviors that are attributed to nature or to biology can thus become reasons for maintaining women in a subordinate position. If men are more aggressive, then they should make better businessmen, lawyers, soldiers, or bankers. Women, if they are more caring, should make better nurses or teachers.

Biological arguments have led to the development of stereotypes that are deeply rooted in Western culture. Small children learn the nursery rhyme: "Sugar and spice and everything nice; that's what little girls are made of" and "sticks and snails and puppy dogs' tails; that's what little boys are made of." Although, of course, no children are actually composed of either one of these sets of materials, the toddler learns at an early age that boys and girls are made of very different ingredients and that while one is perhaps nicer than the other, the other seems, if nothing else, more interesting and adventuresome. As the toddler grows older, if she is a girl, she may feel the need to affirm her gender by avoiding things that are not "nice." Through the ages things that are not nice enough for girls have included careers in law, medicine, and politics.

When higher education for women became a possibility in this country during the nineteenth century, "learned" men offered biological explanations for why women should not be allowed to study. One widely quoted expert on the subject was a Harvard professor, E. H. Clarke. In his book *Sex in Education, or A Fair Chance for Girls,* Clarke wrote, "a girl cannot spend more that four, or, in occasional instances, five hours of force daily upon her studies, and leave sufficient margin for the general physical growth that she must make. . . . If she puts as much force into her brain education as a boy, the brain or the special apparatus (that is, the reproductive system) will suffer."[1]

What is most extraordinary about Dr. Clarke's opinion is that he wrote these words at a time when great numbers of white women in America and virtually all African-American women worked from sunrise to sunset either on farms or in factories. As the European feminist Marie-Louise Janssen-Jurreit writes, "At that time women were already

Women picking cotton in the Mississippi Delta. The "weaker sex" argument was often used in the nineteenth century to relegate women to a second-class status in society. Yet at the same time, women toiled long hours in fields and factories.

employed in brickworks or stamping down stones. They were metalworkers and miners, stitch by stitch they sewed themselves to death at starvation wages; then, as now, they performed the hardest work in the fields. . . . But the female constitution is too delicate—says the patriarch—for the universities to be opened to women."[2]

The biological justification for sex discrimination does not belong to the nineteenth century alone. In the twentieth century men—and women—have argued that each sex excels at certain tasks because of hormonal differences. Others have asserted that differences in brain organization mean that women are better than men at certain kinds of work, and vice versa. The danger in these theories is that for the most part they have been used to justify keeping women in jobs that pay lower wages and have less prestige or power in society. Many Americans, for example, believe that it would be dangerous for a woman to be president because at various points in her menstrual cycle or during pregnancy the flow of hormones might cause her to make irrational decisions. Using biological arguments in this way appears to give sex discrimination "scientific proof" that women cannot do some of the more important and more powerful things that men have done for generations.

Although most of the examples here have been for Americans living in a Western industrial society, sex discrimination is not limited to Western civilizations. Sara Stein has written, "No culture that has been examined fails to make fundamental distinctions between men and women and to express those distinctions in the symbols and structures of their society."[3] The Romans, from whom much of

Western legal tradition is derived, viewed their concept of "paterfamilias" as the natural ordering of society. The *pater,* or father, was the natural head of the *familias,* or family. From this grew the concept that man was the natural head of the government.

It is no accident that the word *patriarchy,* meaning "rule of the fathers," comes from the Latin word for father. In Rome it was the law that a woman was subservient to her father until she was married; at that time her husband usually replaced her father as her master, although in some cases her father retained control over her. For the unmarried woman whose father died, her next closest male relative became, by law, her superior.

The Roman men who made these laws believed that they did so to protect the women in their society. What they perhaps did not realize was that by legalizing women's protection in this way, they were also legalizing the idea that women, by needing the protection of men, were weaker than men and thus less important and powerful in society.

DIVISION OF LABOR

In many societies theories of biological divisions between the two sexes lead to rigid divisions between the kinds of work that men and women do. In many instances the work done by women is extremely backbreaking and strangely at odds with the idea that women are the weaker sex. Among the Tsambigula people of New Guinea, girls are not allowed to play, although boys are, because it is believed that girls must be trained for a lifetime of work. Among Muslims living in Arab villages, women are the carriers. By custom men carry, as one observer noted, "nothing less dignified than a gun."[4] Among the nomads of Tibet, men do all of the needlework, including sewing wedding dresses. Although it might appear that these nomads reverse Western roles—where domestic tasks such as sewing are more likely to fall to women—in fact, this needlework is one of the most valuable products of the Tibetan communities. What is clear from this example is that a society's most valuable or most prestigious tasks belong to men. In preindustrial Europe women were the spinners of thread, and men were the weavers; weaving was considered the more valuable craft.

A biological fact the world over is that there are approximately 105 boys born for every 100 girls. By the age of thirteen in industrial societies, the numbers are equal, and by the age of twenty the girls outnumber the boys. These numbers are consistent across the world.

What has also been consistent is discrimination against women, sometimes in the form of violence. As Janssen-Jurreit has stated, "Physical violence toward women must be regarded as a universal characteristic of human society."[5] In highly industrialized societies such as the United States, violence against women has taken the form of rape and wife-battering. In other nations it has taken the form of infanticide—the murder of infant girls. In areas of the world where poverty is rampant and families often have too many children to feed, baby girls are allowed to die while their brothers are given what food is available. In almost every society boys are worth more. This is certainly true in India. In the Punjab and Kashmir at the beginning of the century, there were tribes in which not one single girl child was left alive. And the Bedees, a branch of the Sikhs, are nicknamed the *koree mar,* or "daughter butchers," because of their violence toward infant daughters.

WOMEN AND RELIGION

Although most Americans would be horrified at the thought of murdering any child, especially on the basis of its sex, the idea of sex inequality is deeply rooted in the religious and intellectual heritage of most Americans. The great male thinkers of Western civilization—from Aristotle to the Jewish patriarchs to the Christian apostles—all assigned women a secondary status, inferior to men. St. Paul wrote that women need to be quiet in church; from his epistle has come a long-standing tradition in Roman Catholicism and certain Protestant sects that women not be ordained as priests and ministers.

Although this second-class citizenship within organized religion has changed dramatically for Protestants in the last twenty years, women are still not allowed to become priests in the Roman Catholic church. And in many Protestant branches of Christianity women face continuing discrimination. In 1970 the Episcopal church allowed the ordination of women, but there are many dioceses that refuse to hire a woman. The Salvation Army claims that it allows women "full equality," but a woman is not allowed to earn more money nor hold a higher rank than her husband. Orthodox Jews maintain strict separation of men and women in religious rituals, with women sitting in the balcony, away

from the center of worship. A daily prayer for Orthodox Jewish men includes the line "I thank thee, Lord, for not having created me a woman." Perhaps most appalling, however, are church doctrines that allow for the physical abuse of women. In the sixteenth century the Eastern Orthodox priest Sylvester advised his male worshipers that "to beat [your wife] carefully with a whip is sensible, painful, fear-inspiring and healthy."

COLONIAL AMERICA

This religious and philosophical position—the inferiority of women—came to the New World on the *Mayflower* and all of the other ships bringing Europeans to the colonies of North America. Most of the early settlers were Protestants, and their theology clearly outlined a secondary status for women. Among the early Protestants in New England, the Calvinists were dominant. The Calvinists emphasized the story of Adam and Eve as explaining the development of "original sin" in humans. Furthermore, they noted that it was Eve, the woman, who ate the apple. From this they developed a number of generalizations about women being more susceptible to evil and the lure of the Devil and thus needing the controlling influence of men. Once in

In 1989, some twenty years after the Episcopal church sanctioned the ordination of women as priests, Barbara Harris of Boston became the church's first woman bishop.

the New World these attitudes were at odds with the necessities of wresting a living out of a wilderness land. For the new Americans, as they would soon be called, the ironies of second-class citizenship were almost immediately apparent. While European men believed that women were physically inferior, they needed the help of women to found the new nation. While men of the era believed that seafaring and adventure were the province of men, they had to entice women to strike out for the new country, or there would be no future generations to people the land.

Throughout the years of colonial settlement, men outnumbered women by an average of three to one. Under these conditions women became more valuable; in any society what is scarce has more value attached to it. In the early 1600s women were often paid to travel to America to become wives. Once there they were forced by economic necessity to do all of the work that men on the frontier had to do. William Byrd, one of the "founding fathers" of Virginia, left this diary account of a colonial Virginia woman: "She will carry a gun in the woods and kill deer, turkeys, etc., shoot down wild cattle, catch and tye hogs, knock down beeves with an axe and perform the most manful exercises as well as most men in these parts."[6]

In addition to doing all of this traditional male work, the colonial woman had an enormously difficult and time-consuming job as a housewife. She had to make the cloth and then sew every stitch of clothing her family wore, including diapers and sheets. She had to cook three meals a day over an open fire. To preserve food from spoiling in an era before refrigeration, she had to can, pickle, and salt enough to last through non-harvest times. All cooking and baking was done over an open fire, and the kettles of boiling water necessary for cooking often weighed thirty or forty pounds. In addition, many women, especially when their husbands died, took on the running of businesses—stores, taverns, inns, and mills.

Yet in spite of this work and the fact that individual men recognized their dependence on women's equal sharing in the development of the new country, the laws that were established to govern the colonies did not reflect the realities of women's equal efforts on behalf of the new nation. In Maryland, for example, a colonial woman, Margaret Brent, proved by her management of her own plantation and that of Lord Calvert, governor of the colony, that she was as adept at managing lands and finances as any man in the colony. It was an era when land ownership meant political power for white males; yet when Margaret Brent asked for a seat in the Maryland Assembly, she was denied.

Colonial women like Margaret Brent represented women's first attempts in Western history to have a say in government. For the next three hundred years, first in the colonies and then in the nation formed from them, many women would continue to strive for political rights. They believed that the right to vote and the right to hold office were essential steps in taking a stand against the sex discrimination that was imported into the country by the first settlers along with the British and European legal systems.

It is important to remember that in these early pleas for equality, and in many of the later stands taken against sex discrimination, the leaders were white upper-class women. Margaret Brent and women like her, although they worked extremely hard and were denied political power that was rightfully theirs, still had a certain degree of independence and economic power. The black woman who lived in the colonies, on the other hand, suffered double discrimination. As a woman she was a second-class citizen, and as a black slave she had no claim to citizenship at all.

For the black woman slave, perhaps the most painful area of discrimination was the wanton disregard for her family shown by the institution of slavery. For a white woman in colonial America, it was an integral part of her second-class status that she be a wife and mother and guardian of hearth and home. The black slave woman had no such untouchable sphere. She herself was the property of her white master. Not only did he control her labor, but in all too many instances he controlled her body as well. Marriage between slaves meant nothing to a white master if he desired a black slave as his mistress. Nor did the black woman have control over her children. They could be sold from her at any time. In the history of sex discrimination in America, there is no bleaker chapter than that of female slaves.

In colonial America even death discriminated between the two sexes. Because the country needed its population to grow and because the death rate among children was so high, women in colonial America were encouraged to have as many babies as possible. Families of ten, twelve, or fourteen children were not uncommon. Nor was it uncommon for women to die in childbirth. An all-too-typical

*The black woman slave had to endure
double discrimination. Her natural rights
as a mother were totally disregarded,
and she had no claim to citizenship.*

epitaph on a Massachusetts tombstone described the dead woman buried beneath it: "She'd fourteen children with her/At the table of the Lord."

If a married woman had much to fear from childbirth, she could find little solace in her legal status. Colonial society greatly encouraged marriage, and single women were objects of pity or ridicule as "spinsters" and "old maids." However, under the law married women had far fewer rights than their single sisters. Discrimination against women was firmly entrenched in the legal system during colonial days. The basis for colonial law was the Common Law of England. Under the civil code of this body of laws the right of an individual to own property was the central principle upon which all other laws were based. A married woman under Common Law practice was designated as a *femme couverte,* a French term meaning that the woman was covered, or protected, by her husband. Husband and wife were treated as one unit for legal purposes. Single women, with no male to protect or "cover" them, had virtually the same right to protect their own property as men did.

For the married woman in colonial America, the Common Law dictated that she had no legal property rights. Upon marriage everything she owned, from her clothing to her kitchen utensils, legally belonged to her husband. If her husband died before her, his property, including perhaps the house they had shared for forty years of married life, passed into the hands of the eldest son. Because a married woman had no property rights, she could not make contracts and could not sue in court. Neither, however, could she be sued. When there was no son to inherit his father's property, the nearest living male relative, instead of the widow, received the inheritance.

The American Revolution was fought in large part to free the colonists from the economic and political restraints imposed on them by Great Britain. It is not surprising that within the climate of revolution some strides were made to redress the gender inequities in the laws. Most of the colonies changed their inheritance laws so that female as well as male children could be their fathers' legal heirs. In addition, most of the colonies passed statutes allowing married women in America important rights that were denied to their counterparts in England. Two such rights were family support from a husband who abandoned his wife and the right of a wife to be protected from physical violence. Having these rights on paper and suing for them in court, however, were—and remain—very different things. Until a woman had the financial means and society's approval for a court appearance, these meant little in reality. Nevertheless, in such colonial statutes lay the seeds of reform that would support the next two centuries of battle against sex discrimination.

THREE

A NEW NATION:
EQUALITY FOR ALL?

Although the colonial interpretation of the Common Law meant more freedom for women in the New World than in the Old World, the irony of the American Revolution is that the freedom on which the new nation was founded was not freedom for all. Among the groups that did not share fully in the liberty promised in revolutionary slogans were men who owned no property, blacks, American Indians, and women of all races and economic conditions. However, colonial women helped win the American Revolution. Some of them believed that they should share in the political freedom of the new country and that they should not be discriminated against.

One of the ways that colonial women had helped win the war was by helping with the boycott of English goods. The money the English made through trade with the colonies was a major reason that Great Britain wanted to maintain control over them. The colonies were extremely rich in natural resources that the "Mother Country" needed. Also, according to British law the colonies were forbidden to purchase certain products from any nation other than England. Because of this rule the colonists had to pay whatever prices British merchants wanted to charge. Tea and British cloth were among the products that the colonists boycotted to protest this British monopoly. Since most colonial women were responsible for meals and for clothing for their families, the women had to agree not to purchase these two staple goods. Many did. As one colonial woman wrote, "Tea I have not drunk since last Christmas, nor bought a new gown. . . . I . . . am now making stockings of American wool for my servants. . . . I know this, that as free I can die but once, but as a slave I shall not be worthy of life."[1] One of her sister patriots wrote, "I hope there are none of us but would sooner wrap ourselves in sheep and goatskin than buy English goods."[2]

Most women who took this sort of stand against the British did not carry their protests further. They did not yet envision a new world free of sex discrimination. However, a few women and some men did see the connection between the oppression of the colonists and the oppression of women in a male-dominated society.

One such group lived in Edenton, North Carolina. The women of Edenton, like women elsewhere in the colonies, boycotted British products. In explaining their boycott, however, these women proclaimed that women as well as men had the right to participate in the political life of the nation. For its time the Edenton Proclamation took a radical stand against sex discrimination. Their suggestion was unusual because no women participated formally in the political system of either the colonies or the mother country.

Although there were no formal avenues for colonial women to exercise political powers, some women whose husbands were colonial political leaders influenced those men a good deal. Their influence, however, was indirect and had no dramatic impact on the formulation of laws for the new nation.

"REMEMBER THE LADIES"

Abigail Adams is a good example of a statesman's wife who saw in the new nation the opportunity to change women's status. In the spring of 1776 she wrote to her husband, John Adams, a Revolutionary leader who would become the second president of the United States, "In the new code of laws which I suppose it will be necessary for you to make, I desire you would remember the ladies and be more generous and favorable to them than your ancestors! Do not put such unlimited power in the hands of husbands. Remember all men would be tyrants if they could. If particular care and attention is not paid to the ladies, we are determined to foment a rebellion, and will not hold ourselves bound by any laws in which we have no voice or representation."[3]

Although John Adams greatly respected his wife's opinion on most subjects, he did not respond favorably to this letter. He wrote of her suggestion, "I cannot but laugh." With no recourse other than persuasion at her command, Abigail Adams was frustrated and unsuccessful in her demand that women be treated better under the laws of the new nation. Adams placated his wife by saying, "You know in practice we are the subjects. We have only the name of masters."[4] This attitude, that women somehow ruled men because of their superior nature, was used time and time again to explain why women did not need the protection of full and equal laws.

Abigail Adams was not the only revolutionary woman who took a stand against sex discrimination. Many colonial women noted the unfairness in an educational system that did not allow women the access to knowledge that men had. In 1790 Judith Sargent Murray wrote that women were not innately inferior to men; men simply had a better education. Murray even suggested that Eve was superior to Adam because, in eating the serpent's apple in the Garden of Eden, Eve was showing a "thirst for knowledge." In an essay entitled "On the Equality of the Sexes," Murray wrote, "If opportunity of acquiring knowledge hath been denied us, the inferiority of our sex cannot be fairly deduced from thence."[5] There were other people who took the position that women needed an education. If they were men, they often argued that women needed an education in order to raise their sons to be better citizens. There were very few who, like Murray, felt that women should be educated so that they could take part fully in all aspects of the new nation.

Yet another Revolutionary wife, Lucy Knox, wife of the Revolutionary leader who became the first secretary of the treasury, wrote to her husband that she hoped he would "not consider [himself] as commander in chief of [his] own house—but be convinced . . . that there is such a thing as equal command."[6] And in 1792 another daughter of the Revolution took a stand against the traditional Protestant marriage ceremony, with its oath that a woman must "love, honor and obey" her husband. Applying the ideals of the Revolutionary War to marriage, this woman wrote: "I object to the word 'obey' in the marriage service. . . . Marriage ought never to be considered as a contract between a superior and an inferior."[7]

When the rebellion that Abigail Adams predicted finally came, women had to overcome these stereotypes of "natural rule" in order to gain supporters for laws guaranteeing political and economic equality. To take a stand for these freedoms meant taking a stand against age-old myths that women naturally ruled within the home and that the balance of power between the sexes would be upset if women had access to power outside their homes.

WOMEN IN THE EARLY NINETEENTH CENTURY

In the new nation economic and political structures definitely discriminated against women. Women did not run for office nor sit on juries nor vote. They could not go to college or become lawyers or doctors or bankers. Although a few women ran their own businesses, this happened most often in remote areas, frequently after a husband had died. For example, women whose husbands had owned general stores or stables or ranches or hardware stores sometimes kept running them after their husbands died.

During the 1820s and 1830s many Americans became concerned with a need to reform the new society. Although the United States was the most democratic place on earth, there were still many people who did not share equally in the new nation. African-Americans, the poor, immigrants, and the mentally ill were just a few of the groups who did not have equal rights in the new nation. By joining in the movements to end discrimination against these various groups, women learned how to organize against discrimination. The tactics they learned would prove to be important strategies in the fight against sex discrimination. In addition, working for the various reform movements allowed some women their first opportunity to work outside the home, in the political and civic arenas that had been closed to them for so long. As part of the protest against England, where taxes supported the Church of England, the new nation had separated the government from religion. Women's activism in reform movements had its roots in the democratically inspired religious Great Awakening that swept the country at the turn of the century. The new churches, with no central means of support, had to depend on the work of the members of their congregations for support. Women provided much of that support. Churches were considered to be proper places for women to volunteer to work outside the home. Women in the churches formed associations to help with charity work.

This organizational experience would prove to

be useful in the reform movement. Women learned to speak at meetings, to raise money, and to run for and elect officers of their associations. They would use these skills in organizations designed to fight prostitution, drunkenness, and slavery in the 1830s and 1840s. Although the majority of these women were white, they would find increasing numbers of African-American supporters as the fight to end slavery grew.

During this same time women found another place outside the home where they could work and even earn a modest wage. The new career open to them was teaching. Although a Massachusetts law as early as 1789 mentioned "school-mistresses" as well as schoolmasters, until the 1830s most school-teachers were male.

One of the growing beliefs of the new nation was that democracy for all meant education for all. For the new democracy to be successful, all voting citizens needed to be able to read and write. If they were not literate, the people would not be able to make informed decisions about electing their leaders. Furthermore, the United States, almost from the beginning, was a nation that prided itself on technology and progress. Shortly after the American Revolution the country had thrown itself fully into the industrial revolution. The new technology that industrialism brought with it meant a need for even more schools and teachers. In the young nation there were simply not enough men to staff all of the schools that were needed.

People who had long opposed the idea of white women working outside their homes quickly developed a rationale for women to become teachers. It was a woman's duty, the argument went, to help the new nation by educating its sons to become good citizens. And for women to be good teachers they would, of course, have to be educated themselves. Consequently, the movement of women into the field of teaching coincided with the growth of schools for girls.

EMMA WILLARD AND THE TROY FEMALE SEMINARY

The most famous of these schools was the Troy Female Seminary in Troy, New York, founded by Emma Hart Willard in 1821. Willard was a far-sighted woman whose husband's financial reserves during the War of 1812 made it necessary for her to earn money to support her family. Emma Willard was frustrated by the fact that she had not had an educational opportunity equal to that of her husband, brothers, and stepsons. While one of her stepsons attended Middlebury College, Emma read his textbooks, especially those in mathematics and science. She found that she was just as capable as he was of understanding the material. She determined that she would provide other young women with a modern education equal to that offered to young

Emma Willard (1787–1870) founded the Troy Female Seminary in Troy, New York, to train women to become teachers as part of an early effort to educate women for careers outside the home.

men. She established a school with a modern curriculum, including higher mathematics and science, subjects not previously taught to young women. In her pioneering school Emma Willard took a stand against sex discrimination.

There had always been schools for girls in the United States, but most of them were academies where girls were taught reading and writing, music, art, and perhaps some French. In addition, the curriculum always stressed the domestic arts: sewing and housekeeping. Girls educated in academies were being groomed for life at home as wives and mothers. At Emma Willard's seminary and at the seminaries founded about the same time by Mary Lyons and Catherine Beecher, women were educated to become teachers. These were the first formal attempts to educate women for a career outside the home. During its first fifty years the Troy Seminary educated twelve thousand young women; perhaps as many as two-thirds of them taught at some point in their lives.

Even in the formation of her school, however, Emma Willard faced significant sex discrimination. In 1819 she wrote a "Plan for Female Education," which still stands as a model for the equal education of women and men. She hoped to persuade the New York State legislature to provide funds to support her school. However, Emma Willard herself, because she was a woman, was not allowed to address the legislature in person.

Believing that Emma Willard's seminary would be a great benefit to their community, the city fathers of Troy, New York, offered a building and $4,000 to begin the venture. However, Emma's husband, John Willard, had to sign the contract because, as a married woman, Emma's signature was not valid.

ELIZABETH CADY STANTON

At the same time that Emma Willard was founding her school, one of her future pupils—and one of the nation's future female leaders—was also learning firsthand of discrimination against women, especially married women. Elizabeth Cady was a young girl who liked to loiter outside her father's law office. One day, as she later recalled in her memoirs, she heard her father speaking to a distraught neighbor woman. The woman, Mrs. Flora Campbell, was a widow who had earned enough money through her own labor as a domestic servant to buy a farm for herself and her husband. When her husband died, the farm passed by his will to her eldest son, who was irresponsible and alcoholic. Judge Cady explained to his daughter that under the law married women's property belonged to their husbands. Husbands could dispose of their wives' property as they saw fit. The fact that Mrs. Campbell's money had purchased the property was irrelevant in the eyes of the law. Young Elizabeth Cady was incensed at the unfairness of the legal system. She determined to fight against sex discrimination and discrimination of all kinds wherever she found it.

Elizabeth Cady Stanton's life paralleled the changes in women's status during the nineteenth century. She was born in time to attend the Troy Female Seminary and was graduated in 1832.

Equally important, she reached her maturity in the 1830s and 1840s at a time when women were beginning to enter public life through the various reform movements that were sweeping the country. The abolition of slavery would be the cause that would take her into the political arena.

In the 1820s state laws had been revised so that almost all white males had the right to vote. Property ownership was no longer a universal requirement for suffrage. As democracy widened, many people questioned why women were not included and why slavery still existed. Black men, as well as women of all colors, clearly did not share in the benefits of the widening franchise. These inequities were obvious to even the most casual observer.

Democracy in America did not yet mean democracy for all. From this realization grew a number of reform movements. None of them was more powerful nor more violent nor ultimately more successful than the abolition movement. And because so many women were so active in the abolition movement, including Elizabeth Cady Stanton, abolitionism became the training ground for thousands of women who would use the tactics they learned in fighting slavery to fight against sex discrimination in the years after the Civil War.

Elizabeth Cady Stanton (1815–1902)
was a key organizer of the
Seneca Falls women's rights
convention held in Seneca
Falls, New York, in 1848.

WOMEN AND ABOLITION

During the 1830s women throughout the Northern states began to form antislavery societies. Although many male northerners were abolitionists, they were often uneasy at having female supporters in their organizations. Women who spoke out in public were easy targets of ridicule. Many men who held quite radical positions on the topic of slavery did not want to be associated with the even more radical topic of equal rights for women. To appear on a public platform with a woman was sure to invite ridicule and scorn for any man in the 1830s. Most of the male abolitionists felt that their cause would be weakened if they allowed women full participation in the antislavery movement. One of the rare exceptions to this was the fiery and extremely radical William Lloyd Garrison. Garrison refused to compromise on any issue—slavery or woman's rights. He believed in immediate emancipation of the slaves and the full participation of women in the abolition movement and other political arenas.

Among the women who took a stand against slavery that was as uncompromising as that taken by William Lloyd Garrison were two sisters from Charleston, South Carolina. Angelina and Sarah Grimké were raised by a slave-owning father and had seen firsthand the horrors of slavery. Determined to speak out on the subject, they contacted Garrison and arranged to travel throughout the North in the winter of 1836–1837 to describe slavery. Originally, they intended their talks for female abolitionists, but they often attracted large crowds of men as well as women.

The Grimkés had been renounced by their

family. In fact Angelina, the older sister, had left home in 1822 to settle in Philadelphia. She had converted to the Quaker religion because the Quakers were abolitionists. However, even the Quakers did not satisfy Angelina, nor her sister Sarah, who had joined her in the North in 1829. The Quakers believed in the gradual and nonviolent freeing of the slaves. The Grimkés were drawn to the more immediate emancipation of slaves that was favored by Garrison. With each hour of delay, they knew another slave was beaten, another slave family was separated, another slave life was ruined. As Angelina wrote, "This is a cause worth dying for."[8]

Although the Grimké sisters initially spoke only against slavery, they quickly had to embrace the "woman question." The presence of female supporters in any reform movement gave rise to what nineteenth-century men referred to as "this woman question." In reforming society what role should women play? How far should democracy be extended? To Angelina and Sarah Grimké the answers to these questions were as simple as the answer to slavery. Slaves should be freed, and women should be given full political and social rights. Increasingly, for them, the two questions became intertwined.

As the Grimkés' lectures became more popular, they moved outside the parlors of female abolitionists and into public lecture halls, where the crowds included men. Even many abolitionists were appalled that women would be bold enough to speak in public. Some female reformers, including Catherine Beecher and Emma Willard, felt that the Grimkés had gone too far. Angelina Grimké replied directly to her critics:

Now I believe it is woman's right to have a voice in all the laws and regulations by which she is governed, whether in church or State: and that the present arrangements of society, on these points, are a violation of human rights, a rank usurpation of power. . . . I contend that woman has just as much right to sit in solemn conventions, conferences, associations and general assemblies as man—just as much right to sit upon the throne of England or in the Presidential chair of the United States.[9]

Sarah Grimké was no less outspoken than her sister. A group of ministers who opposed the women's public appearances had published a *Pastoral Letter,* in which they alleged that the New Testament forbade woman to speak in public and that women who did so would lose their womanly qualities, especially the ability to bear children. In response to the *Pastoral Letter,* Sarah Grimké wrote, "The Lord Jesus defines the duties of his followers. . . . I . . . find him giving the same directions to women as men. . . . Men and women were CREATED EQUAL; they are both moral and accountable beings, and whatever is *right* for a man to do, is *right* for a woman to do."[10]

In taking a public stand against slavery, the Grimkés were forced to take a stand against sex discrimination. Nor were they the only women who found the two causes—slavery and the woman question—similar.

In 1840 abolitionists held a World Anti-Slavery Convention in London. The delegates to the convention voted to exclude women from speaking or voting. Under the circumstances William Lloyd Garrison refused to participate, but most of the male abolitionists in attendance were relieved that the woman question would not ruin the proceedings at the convention. Among the delegates to the conference was Henry Stanton, who had brought with him his young wife, the former Elizabeth Cady. Like the other women in attendance, Elizabeth Stanton had to sit behind a curtain, separated from the main floor where the proceedings were conducted. In true Elizabeth Cady Stanton form, she rankled at the injustice and determined that women should have the right in the future for full public participation in all matters of great importance. During the convention she met and formed a lifelong friendship with Lucretia Mott, a Quaker abolitionist. Mott agreed with Stanton's views on women's exclusion from the World Anti-Slavery Convention, and the two began planning in London for a conference on women's rights.

Even among the abolitionists, few women had the opportunities that Stanton and Mott had to attend public conventions, even conventions where they were separated from the main floor by a curtain. And in spite of reforms, few women had the education of Elizabeth Cady Stanton. However, thousands of women found in the abolition movement the opportunity to learn organizational skills and to form networks of support with other women. They also had the opportunity to learn more about the structure of the government and how to effect social change through political means. Women could not vote or hold office, but they could make their views known through petitions. The

Grimkés alone had gathered the signatures of twenty thousand women who opposed slavery and wanted their views known to state legislators.

In presenting her petitions to the legislature of Massachusetts, Angelina Grimké stated, "I hold, Mr. Chairman, that the American women have to do with this subject [slavery], not only because it's moral and religious, but because it is political."[11] In taking a stand against slavery the reformers of the early nineteenth century were inevitably forced to take a stand against sex discrimination. Women's awakening sense of their need for a political voice, in addition to their new educational opportunities, meant that by 1840 American women were carving a new position for themselves in the society.

=====FOUR=====

"THAT ALL MEN AND WOMEN ARE CREATED EQUAL"

THE SENECA FALLS CONVENTION

In writing about the World Anti-Slavery Convention many years later, Elizabeth Cady Stanton said, "As Mrs. Mott and I walked home, arm in arm, commenting on the incidents of the day, we resolved to hold a convention as soon as we returned home and form a society to advance the rights of women."[1] Stanton and Mott had learned that one effective way of taking a stand on an issue was to hold a convention. They determined to use this strategy in their continuing fight against sex discrimination.

The idea for a convention that was born on the streets of London became a reality in 1848 when Mott, Stanton, and other women, including Lucy Stone, held a woman's rights convention in the small town of Seneca Falls, New York. For some time after their honeymoon in London, Henry and

Elizabeth Stanton had lived in Boston. Bearing and raising young children and surrounded by the rich cultural life of the city, Elizabeth had not had time to plan a convention. But after Henry Stanton moved his family to rural Seneca Falls, Elizabeth found not only time but the added incentive of being a young wife and mother with few outlets of her social and political energy. When her old friend Lucretia Mott happened to visit the area, Stanton and Mott determined to hold a woman's rights convention without further delay. Through the local newspaper they called for a convention to be held in Seneca Falls on July 19 and 20, 1848.

Although many people, including Henry Stanton, felt the convention would be a fiasco, more than three hundred people, most of them women, attended the meeting. James Mott, Lucretia's husband, agreed to chair the proceedings because none of the women had had much experience with parliamentary procedure. Elizabeth Cady Stanton, however, read to the delegates the document for which the Seneca Falls Convention would be remembered: "The Declaration of Sentiments and Resolutions."

THE DECLARATION

Modeled on the Declaration of Independence, the Seneca Falls Declaration began: "We hold these truths to be self-evident: that all men and women are created equal." As self-evident as that truth might have been to the convention-goers, it was a radical stand for 1848. Following the principle of sex equality to its logical conclusion of full participation by women in the political and economic life of the nation created divisions among the Seneca Falls participants.

The declaration elaborated on the theme of equality by likening men's oppression of women to the tyranny of King George III. As the Declaration of Independence had cited the oppressive acts of the king toward the colonists, the Seneca Falls document cited the oppressive acts of men toward women. Stating that "the history of mankind is a history of repeated injuries and usurpations on the part of man toward woman," the Declaration of Sentiments and Resolutions outlined the specific grievances that women had. Among them:

He has never permitted her to exercise her inalienable right to the elective franchise . . .

He has made her, if married, in the eye of the law, civilly dead . . .

He has so framed the laws of divorce, as to what shall be the proper causes, and in case of separation, to whom the guardianship of children shall be given, as to be wholly regardless of the happiness of women . . .

He has monopolized nearly all the profitable employments . . .

He has denied her the facilities for obtaining a thorough education, all colleges being closed against her . . .

He has created false public sentiment by giving to the world a different code of morals for men and women . . .

*He has usurped the prerogative of Jehovah him-
self, claiming it as his right to assign for her a
sphere of action, when that belongs to her conscience and to her God . . .*

*He has endeavored, in every way he could, to
destroy her confidence in her own powers, to
lessen her self-respect and to make her willing to
lead a dependent and abject life.*

This document, written nearly a century and a half
ago, clearly outlines the central issues of sex discrimination, many of which continue to be the focus of sex discrimination protests today. Equality of
employment and education, abortion rights, pornography legislation, alimony, double standards
within the judicial system, and the erosion of psy-
chological well-being by second-class citizenship are
all covered by the general tenets of the Seneca Falls
Declaration.

However, just as there is no universal agreement on these issues in 1990, there was no universal agreement on the principles of the declaration
in 1848. After reading the grievances, Elizabeth
Cady Stanton proposed twelve resolutions covering, among other things, women's rights to free
speech, to sue for divorce, to equality in education
and employment, to own property, and to control

*The Woman's Declaration of Independence
adopted by the Seneca Falls Convention called
for women's rights to sue for divorce, to
equality in education and employment, and
to own property, among others.*

A WOMAN'S DECLARATION OF INDEPENDENCE 1848

ELIZABETH CADY STANTON (1815–1902) After seeing the cruel and unjust treatment of women before the law in the office of her father, Judge Cady, she vowed, even as a child, to find a way to help change these laws. Her marriage to the abolitionist leader, Henry B. Stanton, swept her swiftly into the current of national politics. This laid a firm foundation for the political experience to wage the battle for woman's rights in which she was to become a most inspiring leader. Together with friends, she planned and executed the first Woman's Rights Convention in Seneca Falls, New York, July 19th and 20th 1848. Her life story is truly the history of the Woman's Rights Movement.

Elizabeth Cady Stanton

When, in the course of human events, it becomes necessary for one portion of the family of man to assume among the people of the earth a position different from that which they have hitherto occupied, but one to which the laws of nature and of nature's God entitle them, a decent respect to the opinions of mankind requires that they should declare the causes that impel them to such a course.

We hold these truths to be self-evident: that all men and women are created equal; that they are endowed by their Creator with certain inalienable rights; that among these are life, liberty, and the pursuit of happiness; that to secure these rights governments are instituted, deriving their just powers from the consent of the governed. Whenever any form of government becomes destructive of these ends, it is the right of those who suffer from it to refuse allegiance to it, and to insist upon the institution of a new government, laying its foundation on such principles, and organizing its powers in such form, as to them shall seem most likely to effect their safety and happiness. Prudence, indeed, will dictate that governments long established should not be changed for light and transient causes; and accordingly all experience hath shown that mankind are more disposed to suffer, while evils are sufferable, than to right themselves by abolishing the forms to which they are accustomed. But when a long train of abuses and usurpations, pursuing invariably the same object, evinces a design to reduce them under absolute despotism, it is their duty to throw off such government, and to provide new guards for their future security. Such has been the patient sufferance of the women under this government, and such is now the necessity which constrains them to demand the equal station to which they are entitled.

The history of mankind is a history of repeated injuries and usurpations on the part of man toward woman, having in direct object the establishment of an absolute tyranny over her. To prove this let facts be submitted to a candid world . . . .

Now, in view of this entire disfranchisement of one-half of the people of this country, their social and religious degradation, in view of the unjust laws above mentioned, and because women do feel themselves aggrieved, oppressed, and fraudulently deprived of their most sacred rights, we insist that they have immediate admission to all the rights and privileges which belong to them as citizens of the United States.

In entering upon the great work before us, we anticipate no small amount of misconception, misrepresentation, and ridicule; but we shall use every instrumentality within our power to effect our object. We will employ agents, circulate tracts, petition the state and national legislatures, and endeavor to enlist the pulpit and the press in our behalf. We hope this convention will be followed by a series of conventions embracing every part of the country.

Resolutions

Resolved, That all laws which prevent woman from occupying such a station in society as her conscience shall dictate, or which place her in a position inferior to that of man, are contrary to the great precept of nature, and therefore of no force or authority.

Resolved, That woman is man's equal—was intended to be so by the Creator, and the highest good of the race demands that she should be recognized as such.

Resolved, That it is the duty of the women of this country to secure to themselves their sacred right to the elective franchise . . . .

Resolved, That the speedy success of our cause depends upon the zealous and untiring efforts of both men and women, for the overthrow of the monopoly of the pulpit, and for the securing to woman an equal participation with men in the various trades, professions, and commerce.

Resolved, therefore, That, being invested by the Creator with the same capabilities and the same consciousness of responsibility for their exercise, it is demonstrably the right and duty of woman, equally with man, to promote every righteous cause by every righteous means; and especially in regard to the great subjects of morals and religion, it is self-evidently her right to participate with her brother in teaching them, both in public and private, by writing and by speaking, by any instrumentalities proper to be used, and in any assemblies proper to be held; and this being a self-evident truth growing out of the divinely implanted principles of human nature, any custom or authority adverse to it, whether modern or wearing the hoary sanction of antiquity, is to be regarded as a self-evident falsehood, and at war with mankind.

their own wages. None of these resolutions met much opposition. The twelfth resolution, however, divided the convention. That resolution called for women's right to vote. It too passed, albeit by a small margin.

The right to vote provided the political cause for which Stanton would devote the rest of her life. She would not live to see its ultimate success, however, in spite of her longevity. In fact, only one woman among the signers of the Declaration of Sentiments and Resolutions, a teenager named Charlotte Woodward, lived long enough to vote.

The movement begun at Seneca Falls meant that women and men who opposed sex discrimination were now organized and vocal. Although it would be many years before their cause gained much popular support, there was now a forum through which people could take a stand against sex discrimination. Other people in other localities held local women's rights conventions.

At a national women's rights convention in 1855, Lucy Stone spoke of women's disappointment in a nation, formed on principles of democracy, that had excluded women from the fruits of that democracy. She told the convention, "In education, in marriage, in religion, in everything, disappointment is the lot of woman. It shall be the business of my life to deepen this disappointment in every woman's heart until she bows down to it no longer."

SOJOURNER TRUTH— "AIN'T I A WOMAN?"

At another convention in Akron, Ohio, in 1851, one of the most powerful speakers was a former slave named Sojourner Truth. Sojourner Truth linked her oppression as an African-American with her oppression as a woman. In a stirring speech, she cried out to the convention: "That man over there says that women need to be helped into carriages and lifted over ditches, and to have the best place everywhere. Nobody ever helps me into carriages, or over mud puddles, or gives me any best place. And ain't I a woman? Look at me! I have ploughed and planted and gathered into barns and no man could head me. And ain't I a woman? . . . If the first woman God ever made was strong enough to turn the world upside down all alone, these women together ought to be able to turn it back, and get it right side up again!"

Lucy Stone, Elizabeth Stanton, and Lucretia Mott were typical of the woman's rights reformers of the 1840s and 1850s in that they were prosperous, middle-class, white women. Charlotte Woodward, who was a glovemaker, and Sojourner Truth, a former slave, were less typical. However, Woodward and Truth would come to represent more and more American women for whom taking a stand against sex discrimination was a matter of survival. As the nation industrialized and urbanized during the Civil War years and after, the rights these women demanded became ever more important.

WOMEN AND LABOR

White women had begun to work outside their homes in the early 1820s and 1830s, especially in the New England textile industry. Most women—black and white—who worked outside their own homes in the nineteenth century worked as domes-

tic servants in someone else's home, so their work could not truly be considered public. However, as women moved into the factories of New England, the concept of work for women changed forever. From the 1820s on in the United States, whenever women were needed as a source of labor, their work outside the home was rationalized as service to the nation. This was true for the Lowell factory "girls" of the 1820s and would be true for "Rosie the Riveter" and other factory workers of the 1940s. And in each new phase of women's labor, their work brought them up against new forms of sex discrimination.

The opening of the textile mills in New England after the invention of the spinning jenny, the power loom, and the sewing machine meant that there was a great need for people to work in those mills. Francis Cabot Lowell, founder of Lowell, Massachusetts, a mill town, actively recruited single women to work in his mills. In addition to earning money, these young women would be provided with healthy, profitable employment, ran the argument, until they married and had families of their own. Therefore, because they were women, and it was assumed they would ultimately be cared for by a husband, the mill owners, including Lowell, paid

Sojourner Truth (ca. 1797–1883) gave her famous "Ain't I a Woman" speech to a convention in Akron, Ohio, in 1851. She was a leading spokesperson for black emancipation and women's suffrage.

these women a fraction of what they would have paid men for similar work. Even at these low wages, mill work provided the best income available to a young woman. The other occupations open to them—domestic service, seamstressing, and teaching—paid even less.

The lives of the early female mill workers were not all bad. Although they worked extraordinarily long days for low wages by twentieth-century standards, many of these young women would have worked days that were just as long at tasks that were even harder for no wages had they remained on family farms in Vermont, New Hampshire, or Maine. Working in factories seemed to many of them like a grand adventure. They eagerly left small country towns to go to mill work in the cities. In the beginning these girls were fairly well treated as far as food and housing were concerned. To get New England farmers to allow their daughters to work in the mills, the owners had to prove that they would care for them in much the same way their families had.

The early mill girls, however, encountered a pattern of sex discrimination in employment that would pervade urban America. As immigrant women and, later, freed slave women took the place of white American farm girls, conditions changed dramatically. The Irish were among the first immigrants to flock to the mills. In 1845 only 7 percent of mill workers had been born outside the United States. By 1850, 50 percent had been born in Ire-

Women working in a textile mill, around 1895

land. These Irish women were held in low esteem by the mill owners. Their stereotype of these women was that they were immoral, an assumption they used to argue that it was no longer necessary to guard their morality. This rationalization allowed owners to decline to provide decent housing for them. Furthermore, millions of Irish immigrants were forced to come to America by the potato famine. Any living was better than the certain starvation they had faced in Ireland. In short, it was extremely profitable for New England factory owners to hire these immigrant women: their circumstances ensured they would work for low wages and accept poor conditions.

Employment was gender-segregated from the first, and jobs done by women commanded far lower salaries than those performed by men. Women rarely held supervisory positions. In the hierarchy of the factory, men supervised while women worked. Men held high-paying jobs as mechanics and engineers while women were mere machine operators.

The discrimination in employment that the factory workers faced was evident in other occupations as well. Housemaids earned less than butlers or chauffeurs, and seamstresses earned less than tailors. At a state teachers' convention in Rochester, New York, in 1852, Susan B. Anthony, who would join with Elizabeth Cady Stanton in the fight for votes for women, pointed out the reason that teaching had both low status as a profession and a low salary scale. Addressing the men in the audience who were grumbling about their low pay and low status, Anthony said, "Do you not see that so long as society says a woman is incompetent to be a lawyer, minister or doctor, but has ample ability to be a teacher, that every man of you who chooses this profession tacitly acknowledges that he has no more brains than a woman. And this, too, is the reason that teaching is less a lucrative profession, as there men must compete with the cheap labor of women."[2]

Susan B. Anthony firmly believed that as long a women did not have the full citizenship rights of men, their labor would be devalued. Gaining the vote, she argued, was the first and most important step in achieving economic, political, and social equality for women.

RECONSTRUCTION AND VOTES FOR WOMEN

The Civil War accelerated industrialism and opened up new careers for women, but it did little to change occupational discrimination. As the factories of the North turned to providing boots and uniforms and canned foods for the federal troops, more and more women were drawn to factory work.

One totally new career emerged for women during the Civil War: nursing outside the home. Although women had long been the primary caregivers in their families, nursing strangers was considered disreputable work. "Normal" women were considered too modest and refined to bathe and dress strange men. The number of war wounded, however, meant that there was a terrible shortage of nurses. Dorothea Dix, a woman who had been active in the 1830s in reform movements for better care of the mentally ill and physically impaired, was

appointed superintendent of nurses for the federal government.

In her first appeal for nurses, Dix reflected the double standard that most nineteenth-century Americans applied to men and women. She hired only women over thirty and only those who were "plain in appearance," fearing that younger, more attractive women might be corrupted by their intimate contact with strange men. In spite of her requirements, women of all ages and all physical types heeded Dix's call and hurried to war hospitals to help tend the wounded. Among them was Louisa May Alcott, who would later become the most famous children's book author in the country. In her war diary Alcott chafed at the inferior status of the nurses and the discriminating treatment they received at the hands of the male doctors.

When the war ended, women did not retreat from nursing but claimed it as their own special occupation. One of the first women doctors in the country, Elizabeth Blackwell, had trained hundreds of army nurses. Her methods were regularized after the war. Hospitals established schools of nursing to provide more ongoing training and professional standards. The work of another army nurse, Clara Barton, led to her establishment of the American Red Cross, a neutral medical and service corps providing comforts to all who needed them in times of war or natural disaster.

Elizabeth Cady Stanton (left) and Susan B. Anthony (right) in a photo taken around 1881.

By the twentieth century well over 90 percent of all professional nurses were women, and nursing had joined teaching as an acceptable occupation for women. Like teaching, however, nursing was devalued. Salaries were extremely low, particularly in comparison to those of doctors, nearly all of whom were male. The establishment of nursing as a woman's occupation and the discrepancy between nurses' salaries and salaries for comparable work done by men would continue for over a century and lead to a critical nursing shortage in the late twentieth century.

The Civil War initially brought about a change in the work patterns for African-American women as well as white women. Ironically, for the ex-slave, freedom meant the freedom to work inside one's own home. Slave women for too long had had to work in the master's house and at tasks in the master's fields that most nineteenth-century Americans—black and white—felt were better suited to men. The first years of freedom for many ex-slave women meant the freedom to establish their own homes.

However, the economic reality of racial discrimination meant that for their families to survive, the freed women had to work for low wages as domestic servants or field hands for their former masters. Most freed slaves remained in the South, where the twin prejudices of gender and race were most pervasive. Frequently, black women found it easier to earn wages outside their homes, especially as maids, than their husbands could.

During the Reconstruction period—the years immediately following the Civil War—politicians wrestled with the establishment of civil and political rights for African-Americans. The Republican party held a clear majority and gradually evolved a plan that would lead to two constitutional amendments granting all male Americans equal civil rights, including the right to vote. Few male Americans of either race believed that the franchise should be extended to women.

For women like Elizabeth Cady Stanton, Sojourner Truth, and Susan B. Anthony, who had labored so long against both racial and sex discrimination, the unwillingness of the Republican leaders to include women in the Fourteenth and Fifteenth amendments was a bitter blow. Just as abolitionists had feared that the "women question" would scare away too many of their supporters, so too did the Reconstruction senators and congressmen fear that votes for women would defeat the amendment for black suffrage.

The Civil War had meant the widening of women's opportunity, but in addition it had brought about new areas of sex discrimination. For example, women in urban areas whose wages were so low that they could not enjoy a decent standard of living were excluded from the new trade unions forming in industrial America. And certainly no group needed more protection under the law than African-American women. As Stanton asked, "My question is this: Do you believe the African race is composed entirely of males?" Sojourner Truth echoed this sentiment when she said, "There is a great stir about coloured men getting their rights but not a word about coloured women; and if coloured men get their rights and not coloured women theirs, you see, coloured men will be masters over the women."[3]

THE SUFFRAGISTS

The failure of the Fourteenth and Fifteenth amendments to include women redirected the woman's rights movement after the war. Women who took a stand against sex discrimination narrowly focused their campaign on suffrage—the right to vote. By the 1860s, however, there were enough women leaders that a division occurred among the supporters of woman suffrage.

On the one hand were Susan B. Anthony and Elizabeth Cady Stanton, who formed the National Women's Suffrage Association (NWSA) in 1869. In spite of their fervent work as abolitionists, Stanton, Anthony, and their followers in the NWSA refused to support the Fifteenth Amendment, which gave voting rights to all men regardless of race. Believing that any amendment that excluded women was wrong, they vowed to work for a national suffrage law that would include all adults, in spite of race or gender.

Other suffragists, as they soon became known, supported the Fifteenth Amendment because they believed that African-Americans deserved some immediate political rights if the work of the Civil War was not to be undone. In addition, that group, led by Lucy Stone, formed the American Woman Suffrage Association (AWSA), which pledged to work for woman suffrage on the state level.

Another basic difference between the two groups was ideological. The AWSA focused solely on the right to vote. The NWSA, on the other hand, viewed suffrage as the tip of the iceberg of women's oppression. Far more radical in their approach, Stanton and Anthony supported a newspaper called *The Revolution* that covered controversial topics, including women's right to divorce. In addition, Stanton and Anthony tried, for the most part unsuccessfully, to gain support from working women. Their inability to gain much support from these women stemmed from their inability to see how class differences as much as gender differences affected the conditions of working women's lives.

The NWSA and the AWSA remained two separate organizations until 1890, when they merged as the National American Woman Suffrage Association (NAWSA). One of the leaders of the merger was Alice Stone Blackwell, Lucy Stone's daughter and member of a new generation of suffragists. However, the first and second presidents of the new organization, Elizabeth Cady Stanton and Susan B. Anthony, were members of the old guard.

In many ways Stanton and Anthony had not changed at all. Their stand against sex discrimination remained consistent and radical. In 1892 Stanton, after years of hearing from her opponents that the Christian Bible justified sex discrimination, countered by writing *The Woman's Bible*. Beginning with Genesis and proceeding to the Book of Revelations, Stanton explained that the Bible was a book written by man, not God, and that its many anti-female parts were, at the very least, open to inter-

Over (above): A 1915 women's suffrage parade in New York City; (below) Suffragists at the White House gate; (right) A suffrage flagbearer.

TO THE ENVOYS OF RUSSIA.

President Wilson and Envoy Root are deceiving Russia.
They say,"we are a democracy. Help us win a world war
so that democracies may survive."

We, the Women of America, tell you that America is not a democracy.
Twenty million American Women are denied the right to vote.
President Wilson is the chief opponent of their national enfranchisement.

Help us make this nation really free. Tell our government that it must
liberate its people before it can claim free Russia as an ally.

pretation. By challenging the scriptural support for sex discrimination, Stanton took the most controversial position of a long and controversial career. Most of the members of the NAWSA disagreed with Stanton, but by this point, woman suffrage had enough support that the organization was able to weather the storm.

As the NAWSA entered the twentieth century under Susan B. Anthony's leadership, votes for women took on a new urgency and gained a new base of support. Progressive Americans in a new century were willing in greater numbers than ever to take a stand against sex discrimination, at least in the form of voting rights.

=FIVE=

THE TWENTIETH CENTURY: FROM THE NINETEENTH AMENDMENT TO THE ERA

The merger of the NWSA and the AWSA into the National American Women Suffrage Association in 1890 reflected the growing solidarity of women—at least white middle- and upper-middle-class women. As the nineteenth century gave way to the twentieth century, industrialization, urbanization, and immigration—forces that had shaped American society for one hundred years—accelerated sharply. Cities grew rapidly, the frontier was officially declared closed, thousands of young people moved from farms to cities, and millions of immigrants, most of them non-English-speaking and non-Protestant, flooded into the United States.

WOMEN IN THE PROGRESSIVE ERA

As a whole, the country welcomed these changes as proof of vitality and progress. In fact, the first years of the twentieth century came to be known as the Progressive Era. Progress seemed to be everywhere and was visible to even the most casual observer in such areas as electricity, streetcars, telegraphs, telephones, and, by 1910, automobiles. America was the land of the future. Thousands of American homes now had gas stoves, indoor plumbing, and electric lights. Clothes could be bought "ready-made," food was now available in cans from grocery stores, and many homes had iceboxes.

Added to the technological inventions were innovations in medicine. Scientists agreed that germs caused disease and set about successfully preventing many illnesses that had wiped out entire families a generation before. The government took a more active role in regulating the products of the new industries. Meat and milk came under government inspection. The regulatory arm of the state and federal governments began to grow. Bureaucracy was on the rise.

The idea that people, working through the American government, could perfect every aspect of the society was almost universally believed by the end of the first decade of the new century. No social problem seemed so great that it could not be solved by American inventiveness, organization, and democracy. America was the biggest, the richest, the most forward-looking of all nations. Immigrants from the Old World came to get a fresh start, to shed old ways, and to make their fortunes or at least secure a better future for their children and grandchildren.

Women found unique opportunities in the Progressive Era. Throughout the nineteenth century, Americans had fashioned a notion of woman as the purer sex. Women, they believed, were gentler, nobler, more virtuous, more moral than men. This argument had been used to keep women out of public life. Now women turned this argument to their advantage. They claimed that the nation needed women's special virtues in this time of change. If women were indeed more moral and more virtuous, then certainly they had an important role to play in perfecting the new society. Twentieth-century America should not only be bigger, wealthier, and more industrialized. It should also be the most humane and most just society on earth. To ensure that these qualities were part of the new America, women should be given the right to vote.

At the same time, the new America called for workers in a variety of new fields. Women had begun to attend college in the 1870s; by 1880 women accounted for 32 percent of all students enrolled in colleges and universities, and by the twentieth century they accounted for close to half of all college students. Half of this college-educated group of women would never marry, and most of them would follow careers in service occupations. As nurses, doctors (especially obstetricians and pediatricians), teachers, and social workers, they would play a vital role in reforming American society along the progressive lines of the era. Along the way they would organize to fight for women's right to vote.

THE SETTLEMENT HOUSE MOVEMENT

The settlement house movement was an important aspect of women's work during this time and characterizes the changing role for women. Beginning in the 1890s, educated women founded houses in urban slum areas to provide education and cultural centers for the thousands of immigrant women living in poverty in American cities. The most famous of these was Hull House, founded in Chicago by Jane Addams and Ellen Gates Starr. The purpose of Hull House was to Americanize immigrant women. Believing that everything American was better, the settlement house workers felt that the more quickly immigrants learned to speak English and to follow American customs, the faster American society would progress.

Women like Addams and Starr were college-educated and lived apart from their families. They assumed public roles and were outspoken champions of their settlement houses. They saw the need for women's votes in order to influence legislation on housing, employment, child and woman labor, and the host of new laws regulating food and medicine. They believed that the spheres traditionally assigned to women—home and children—were increasingly affected by the modern age. To maintain control over their traditional spheres, women needed to be able to vote. For example, a woman in the nineteenth century had usually known, even if she lived in the city, what farm her family's meat and milk came from, so she had some notion of the purity of the food she fed her family. As great meat-packing industries centralized meat production, however, women lost immediate control over

Jane Addams (1860–1935), American social reformer, in a photo taken in 1914.

Hull House in Chicago, the settlement house founded by Jane Addams. Settlement houses provided educational and social service programs for immigrant women.

what their families were eating. They needed the vote in order to support or even initiate regulatory legislation that would help them ensure that the food their families were eating was good food.

Jane Addams specifically supported woman suffrage as a way that women could control their homes and their children's food. In an article for the *Ladies' Home Journal* in 1910, entitled "Why Women Should Vote," Addams wrote: "If the street is not cleaned by the city authorities, no amount of private sweeping will keep the tenement free from grime; if the garbage is not properly collected and destroyed, a tenement mother may see her children sicken and die of diseases from which she alone is powerless to shield them . . . she cannot even secure untainted meat . . . unless the meat has been inspected by city officials. . . . In short, if woman would keep on with her old business of caring for her house and rearing her children, she will have to have some conscience in regard to public affairs lying outside her home."

During the Progressive Era two groups of women joined together to take a stand in favor of votes for women. Some of them were "new women," college-educated and career-minded. Most, however, were traditional white middle-class women who believed, along with their husbands and fathers, that "woman's place is in the home." Fearing that their homes were no longer theirs to control in an urbanized society, they argued for the right to vote as a means of regaining control over their traditional domestic spheres. They wanted to be able to vote for legislation that would ensure that their new electrical appliances were safe, that their modern gas stoves had properly installed valves, that the ingredients in their canned foods matched what the labels said.

Supporting woman suffrage was only one way of taking a stand against sex discrimination during the Progressive Era. There were still many other forms that sex discrimination took in this era. There was as yet little work available to women, and all work for women—whether in factories or in schools—paid less than similar work for men. An immigrant woman who needed to work to supplement her family's income had to work fourteen to sixteen hours, six days a week, to keep her children from starving. Often children worked too, for wages that were even lower than their mother's, but their few pennies bought the bread that kept families from going to bed hungry. When a father was injured or killed at work, which happened all too often before safety regulations were imposed on the new industries, there was no accident insurance or life insurance to help his family. On the one hand, society said that women were not to work outside the home, but conditions in urban America made it impossible for most poor women to stay home and care for their children.

Conditions for working women brought new allies into the suffrage movement. Many women suffrage advocates became champions of legislation that would limit the working day to eight hours and the work week to six days, regulate the wages paid to women, prohibit child labor, and provide a government system of accident and life insurance. The members of the NAWSA saw in the needs of the new industrial society an even greater need for votes for women. As one speaker said at an annual NAWSA convention, "The instant the State took upon itself any form of educative, charitable or personally helpful work, it entered the area of distinctive feminine training and power, and therefore became in need of the service of woman."[1]

THE SUFFRAGE MOVEMENT GROWS

After 1910 the movement for woman suffrage accelerated on the local level. Young women, not content to work through the NAWSA, began grassroots movements in the states that were designed to unite working women of all classes with the old-line suffragists. Using these methods, by 1910 women had won the right to vote in Washington State and succeeded the next year in California. Kansas, Oregon, and Arizona followed in 1912. In some of these state fights the traditional suffragists found strong allies in working-class women who had fought for union membership in male-dominated unions. These veterans of fights against sex discrimination in unions had an arsenal of tactics that the suffragists put to good use. In the battle against sex discrimination in politics, for example, suffragists used leaflets and pickets. In addition, they learned from union women how to speak effectively in front of large groups. Mass labor meetings had been an effective training ground for women speakers.

For women factory workers the right to vote was urgent. Their leaders scoffed at the idea that voting was an unladylike action, fit only for men.

As one put it, "We have women working in foundries, stripped to the waist [who] . . . stand for thirteen or fourteen hours in the terrible steam and heat. . . . Surely these women won't lose any more of their beauty and charm by putting a ballot in a ballot box once a year than they are likely to lose standing in foundries or laundries all year round."[2]

Sensing that new and greater numbers of women supported the right of women to vote, Carrie Chapman Catt, who had assumed the presidency of the NAWSA in 1915, developed a strategy for the passage of a constitutional amendment giving women the right to vote. Her goal was to achieve the passage of such an amendment by 1920.

Catt combined the grass-roots tactics that had earned suffrage in western states with a campaign for a national amendment. State campaigns were vital in states where women already had the vote. In these areas the suffragists pressed women voters to pass referenda that would bring the constitutional amendment to Congress. In other states, especially states in the conservative South, the organizers worked for state laws that would permit woman suffrage. Both tactics worked.

In 1918, Jeannette Rankin, U.S. representative from Montana and the first woman to be elected to Congress, introduced a constitutional amendment for woman suffrage. By a close vote of 174 to 136, only 1 vote more than the required two-thirds majority, the amendment passed the House of Representatives. Although it took eighteen months, the amendment did pass in the U.S. Senate and was finally ratified by the necessary thirty-six states in August 1920, just in time for that fall's presidential election. The wording of the amendment was direct: the right to vote could not be denied on account of sex.

WOMEN IN THE 1920s

In the two decades after 1920, sex discrimination in American life no longer commanded the attention of the majority of the people. With voting rights and the prosperity of the 1920s, American women seemed to be fully a part of the modern age. The promise of the Progressive Era suffragists had been fulfilled. American women in the 1920s were the freest women anywhere on earth.

The symbol of the American woman of that decade was the "flapper." Although the vast majority of American women were not flappers, radio and the movies—the pioneers of twentieth-century mass media—presented the flapper as the woman of the post–World War I age.

Flappers were unconventional and free. They cut their hair, wore makeup and short skirts, went out at night alone to meet men, smoked cigarettes, and drank alcohol. Since all of this behavior had been forbidden to "nice women" before 1920, the flapper gave the impression that women no longer had any restrictions just because they were women. The magazines, movies, and radio shows that featured flappers as heroines did not focus on the continuing inequities in women's work and pay. Nor did the flapper, once she married, continue to live an unconventional or free life. In fact, the attraction of the flapper to millions of housewives was that as a single woman she could do many things that married women could not do. Bound by economics and tradition, most cared for home and family and did not work outside the home.

WOMEN IN THE 1930s

What married women could not do by custom became legalized during the Great Depression of the 1930s. During that decade the number of married women working outside the home grew by 4 percent. They achieved this increase against incredible odds. The Depression of the 1930s hit everyone. As men, the major breadwinners in most families, lost their jobs, women went out to work to support their families. (It should be noted that black married women had always had to work outside their homes, in far greater numbers than white women did, in order to supplement the substandard wages available to black men.)

As soon as numbers of women began looking for jobs during the Depression, many states and the federal government passed laws discriminating against women. Taking the position that what jobs were available belonged to men, the state legislatures in twenty-six states passed laws prohibiting married women from working. These women, the male legislators firmly believed, had husbands who could and should provide for them. The federal government prohibited more than one member of a family from working in a civil service position. This law most often applied to wives. A poll taken in 1935 found that over half of the American people felt that women should not have jobs if their husbands earned more than $1,000 annually.

The numbers of working women, both single

and married, increased during the Depression in spite of these attitudes and legislation. The reason was sex discrimination of a less obvious but more pervasive form. Many categories of jobs had become almost exclusively female and were so low-paying that men, even in the depths of the Depression, were not anxious to fill them. An example of this was secretarial work.

Before the twentieth century, secretaries were male. They were usually well educated and handled correspondence and bookkeeping for their bosses. The invention of two machines changed the business world and secretarial work forever: the telephone and the typewriter. With these two machines the volume of communications within and among businesses increased rapidly. Platoons of young women were hired to manage switchboards and to fill typing "pools." This "white-collar" work quickly became the province of women, most often young, single women who were working for a short time before marriage. The flappers by night were often secretaries by day. Their salaries were extremely low and remained low because the job was invariably a "woman's job." Many employers, almost invariably men, believed that secretaries did not need to earn much because all of their money was spending money used to fuel their fun until marriage.

However little they were paid, most women with jobs during the Depression decade of the 1930s were subjected to a good deal of hostility from men who were out of work. A typical letter to a U.S. representative from one of his male constituents in 1931 read: "If less women were employed it would make room for the employment of many

Women entered the work force in large numbers as secretarial and clerical workers in the early part of the twentieth century.

of the idle men in our country. . . . I do not believe we are again going to have normal and prosperous times until women do return to their homes."[3]

WOMEN AND WORLD WAR II

Ten years later, Americans totally reversed their feeling about women working outside the home. The Japanese attacked Pearl Harbor on December 7, 1941, and the United States entered World War II. Overnight thousands of American men were mobilized for war. As they headed for the Pacific and European theaters of war, factories at home geared up to produce guns, airplanes, tanks, and other heavy machines necessary for the Allied war effort. There were far more jobs than there were people to fill them. Most of these jobs were considered male jobs.

Quickly, the U.S. government began a campaign to encourage women to take on jobs that had once been considered appropriate only for men. Furthermore, married women were urged to take factory jobs and to work outside the home. The new symbol of American womanhood was "Rosie the Riveter," a glamorous, patriotic woman wielding a hammer or blowtorch, building planes and ships to help bring her man home safely from the war.

A factory recruitment film produced in 1943 was titled *The Glamour Girls of 1943*. The narrator intoned, "Instead of cutting the lines of a dress, this woman cuts the pattern of aircraft parts. Instead of baking cake, this woman is cooking gears to reduce the tension in the gears after use."

Women flocked to the war plants. For the first

time ever they were encouraged to take on skilled, high-paying jobs in heavy industry. By the end of the war six million women had taken on jobs outside their homes, increasing the percentage of women in the work force from 25 to 36. Nor did women limit their work to factories. The absence of men meant that other jobs also opened up for women. Women became truck drivers, bus drivers, and members of local police forces.

Significantly, the women who entered the labor force during World War II differed from the single women who had characterized the working woman before the war. More than half of the women who took jobs outside the home during the war were married, and most of them had young children. Fro the first time the number of married women working outside the home was greater than that of single women. Federal regulations helped women's pay scales stay equal with men's, and federal guidelines on day care underlined the nation's approval for working mothers to find jobs outside their homes.

As soon as the war ended, however, the government attitude and the attitudes of many Americans changed dramatically. Nearly two million women were fired from their factory jobs within a year of V-J Day. Women were told through the media that "real women" would return to their jobs as wives and mothers as soon as the soldiers and sailors returned to peacetime jobs. When women did not voluntarily leave their jobs, they were fired or moved back into more traditional, lower-paying women's jobs.

Unbelievably, women who had been praised by the president and the press for driving cranes, riv-

*During World War II large numbers of women entered
the manufacturing sector of the work force in wartime industries.*

eting ships, and building planes were told that factory jobs in peacetime America were unsuitable for women. When women who had been laid off appealed to the federal government for new jobs, they were shocked to find that skilled industrial jobs paying high wages were no longer open to them. These jobs were reserved for the returning servicemen. Sex discrimination in the workplace was firmly back in place.

WOMEN SINCE WORLD WAR II

In the immediate postwar era, working-class women felt this discrimination most keenly, and their voices were the least readily heard. Many of the white middle-class women who had taken jobs "for the duration" were eager to return home. The "baby boom" of the late 1940s and 1950s is proof that many of these women concentrated on raising young children. The media celebrated life in the suburbs. Elementary school children read of Dick and Jane, who lived in a comfortable house with Mother, who cooked and cleaned and cared for them, and Father, who left for work each morning and returned to his family each night.

In countless homes across the United States

After World War II, women for the most part returned to the home. Mass media created the idealized fifties housewife who just couldn't do without a seemingly endless stream of consumer products.

Betty Friedan, in her 1963 book, The Feminine Mystique, *exploded the view that women must fulfill the narrow roles of housewife and mother.*

women found their roles as suburban housewives unfulfilling. As the 1950s gave way to the 1960s, change was in the air for many parts of American society. African-Americans united in a long-overdue stand against racial inequality. Within the decade more barriers to racial equality would topple than in the entire century since Reconstruction.

A book exploded in this climate of social change and altered Americans' thinking about sex discrimination. Betty Friedan, a housewife frustrated by the narrow roles of wife and mother thrust upon her by 1950s society, wrote *The Feminine Mystique* in 1963. Friedan wrote, "The feminine mystique says the highest value and the only commitment for women is the fulfillment of their own femininity . . . their own nature which can find fulfillment only in sexual passivity, male domination, and nurturing maternal love." Friedan asserted that, through the media, American men assigned to women whatever roles best suited the male view of society at any given point. Although women had the right to vote, the right to hold office, and access to higher education and most professions, the reality was that most women were limited, by subtle and overt sex discrimination, to being wives and mothers.

Women all over the country resonated to Friedan's work. The civil rights movement and the debacle in Vietnam further fueled their thinking that American society, long dominated by white males, needed to be reordered. Chief among the areas that needed rethinking was woman's role in the society. A movement for the adoption of a constitutional amendment outlawing sex discrimination grew in the late 1960s and early 1970s.

The proposed Equal Rights Amendment (ERA) stated: "Equality of rights under the law shall not be denied or abridged by the United States or any state on account of sex." In spite of fervent support by thousands of women and men, the ERA fell short of the number of states needed for ratification. Its opponents successfully argued that the amendment was too radical, that it would force unnatural equality and be too costly.

Although the national ERA failed, many states enacted their own amendments. The federal government in the 1970s vigorously prosecuted a number of sex discrimination cases under Title VII of the Civil Rights Act of 1964 and Title IX of the Education Act of 1972. For example, in 1971 the Supreme Court found invalid an Idaho law that favored male executors over female executors of estates. In 1975 Colorado's highest court ruled that a girl could practice and play with a boys' athletic team when a sport was unavailable to her. In 1974 Illinois overturned a law setting different ages for juvenile status of boys (seventeen) and girls (eighteen).

Nor were all cases of sex discrimination limited to women. In 1974 Illinois ruled that child custody should be determined according to the best interests of the child, rather than placing children with mothers on the grounds that women are better, more natural parents. In 1975 Pennsylvania's high court ruled that a woman was as responsible for her husband's medical care as a husband was for his wife's.

What all of these decisions said was that sex discrimination had no legal justification and that gender should not be a factor in determining the legal rights of either men or women. The Ameri-

*A 1977 rally for the Equal Rights Amendment to the
United States Constitution. The amendment was never ratified.*

Above: An "Anti-Bra Day" protest, 1969.
Opposite: National Organization of Women (NOW) president
Eleanor Smeal speaks on behalf of the ERA.

can Civil Liberties Union took a stand in favor of the ERA and against sex discrimination, saying, "Sex-based laws are unjust and irrational because they use gender rather than ability or need to determine an individual's rights, responsibilities and benefits. The effect of sex-based laws is to steer people into sex tracks and to deny them freedom to choose the path of their own capacities and aspiration."[4]

As the Supreme Court and state courts began to dismantle discriminatory laws in the 1970s, women and men became increasingly aware of the pervasiveness and complexity of sex discrimination in American society. Although antisuffragists had argued that giving the vote to women was an attack on the family, few had taken their charges seriously. New stands against sex discrimination, however, seemed truly to attack traditional family values. Comparable worth, abortion rights, subsidized day care, and maternity or paternity leave seemed to many to weaken the family as a foundation of modern society. To millions of others, however, taking a stand against sex discrimination meant taking a stand on a whole host of women's issues in order to build a new gender-free society.

══════SIX══════

TAKING A STAND AGAINST SEX DISCRIMINATION TODAY

Many Americans, looking at the role played by women in the United States today, have concluded that sexism and sex discrimination are no longer a part of American society. They are wrong. Although it is less pervasive in the United States than in many other nations of the world, sex discrimination still exists. Many battles remain to be fought by younger generations.

THE CHANGING FAMILY

The complexity of sex discrimination has become more apparent as the most obvious barriers to women's full participation in the political and economic life of the country have toppled. Because of women's traditional roles as wives and mothers, taking a stand against sex discrimination during the past two decades has seemed to many people to be taking a stand against families. To some, women's equal sta-

One facet of the changing American family will likely be an increased responsibility for child care on the part of fathers.

tus outside the home has meant that the traditional family—the so-called nuclear family of mother, father, and children—is being destroyed.

In 1978 Jane Howard wrote: "Families aren't dying. . . . What families are doing . . . is changing their size and shape and purpose. . . . Only 16.3% of this country's 56 million families are conventionally 'nuclear,' with breadwinning fathers, home-making mothers, and resident children. That leaves 83.7% to find other arrangements."[1] Often the other arrangements involve single mothers, single fathers, working mothers, fathers who work at home, and a whole host of other relationships that reflect society's changing views of appropriate roles for men and women.

Often, too, the problems in modern society reflect how little society has changed and how much sex discrimination still prevails. For example, there is no profession closed to women today. However, among professional and managerial women aged thirty-five to forty-four, more than one quarter have no children, according to a 1986 study, and other reports put the number even higher. The reason for this has been nicknamed the "Mommy Track." In many corporations, having small children removes a woman from serious consideration for promotion during her late twenties and early thirties, years when most men are busy climbing the ladder of success.

To have young children at home is not seen as a career barrier for men because they are often assumed to have wives who will carry out the traditional duty of raising young children. Working extra-long hours and taking impromptu business trips are the kinds of things that are difficult for people with primary responsibility for children. Children need to be picked up at day care and school at regular times; they need to stay home and be tended when they are sick; they need adult attention and love at mealtimes and bedtimes. Small children's needs have long been primarily the responsibility of women. Small children's needs do not mesh well with the career paths of most professions—law, medicine, business. Until the corporate world makes significant changes in its work patterns, children and their needs will continue to be a focus for sex discrimination in the work world. As long as employers continue to ask otherwise qualified women—but not men—when they plan to start having a family, sex discrimination prevails.

In a poll taken by the *New York Times* in August 1989, "equality on the job" was mentioned most frequently as "the most important problem that faces women today." Although more than half of all American women are now paid for work outside their homes, women earn only 64 percent of what men earn. On the average, women with bachelor's degrees can expect to earn less than a man who is a high school dropout. Access to higher education

There are pros and cons to the "Mommy Track." Some argue that it allows women to start a career, then raise a family, and finally reenter the work force with solid experience under her belt. Others say it is outright discriminatory.

for girls, still considered by many to be less important than for boys, is actually more important for girls in lifetime economic terms.

SEX DISCRIMINATION
IN THE WORKPLACE

One of the most harmful examples of continuing sex discrimination can be found in the types of work women do. Jobs that are filled predominantly by women are usually low-paying. For example, although there are no legal or educational barriers to women's becoming bankers, only 3 percent of the senior management positions in banking are filled by women, a statistic that has not changed in nearly forty years. Although 50 percent of the people now attending law school are women, very few women become partners in major firms. Women are more likely to hold lower-paying legal jobs as assistants and associates.

Banking and the law remain male jobs. Other jobs, especially education, are dominated by women, but again the more highly paid the position, the more likely that the job will go to a man. High school teachers on the whole make more money than elementary school teachers, and college professors make more money than high school teachers. There is more prestige associated with teaching in colleges than in high schools and in high schools than in elementary schools. Administrators at each level make more money and have more job prestige than the faculty they supervise. As the age of students rises, the percentage of women on the faculty and in administrative positions declines accordingly.

Eighty percent of all elementary school teachers are women, but 12 percent of elementary school principals (a much more prestigious, higher-paying position) are women. Fifty percent of all secondary school teachers are women, but only 6 percent of secondary school principals are women. Twenty-nine percent of all college faculty members are women, but only 7 percent of college presidents are women.

Historical evidence underlines the fact that prestige and money influence who gets what job in education. Until the 1950s more than 90 percent of elementary school principals were women. Then, in the cold-war years, as America turned to its schools to help with the technological race against the Soviet Union, a decision was made to "upgrade" elementary education and to pay higher salaries to elementary school administrators. The job became more valuable. By 1970 only 37 percent of elementary school principals were women. The job pattern in education clearly reflects sex discrimination.

Ann Scott of the State University of New York at Buffalo analyzed the breakdown between men and women at the university level. She found that women made up 50 percent of the freshman class, 21 percent of the graduate students, 14 percent of the faculty, and 5 percent of the full professors. She concluded that "men train women into professions in which they are unwilling to hire women as colleagues and as equals."[2]

Over: More and more women are working in traditionally male-dominated areas.

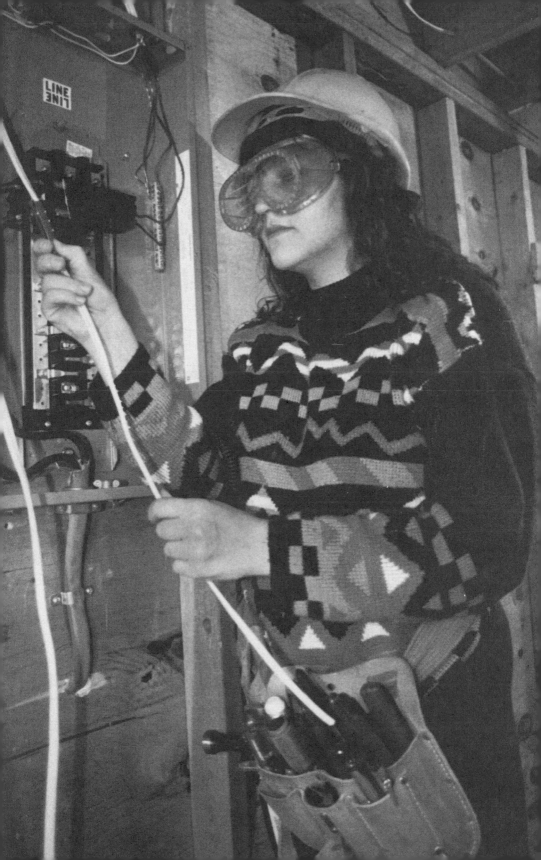

What is true for women in education is true for women in other professions, such as nursing, social work, and secretarial positions. All of these professions are dominated by women, and all of them remain relatively low-paying and low-status.

Behind the continuing sex discrimination in employment is a series of fundamental beliefs about women and work that is just beginning to be understood and challenged. In 1985 Patricia Lengermann and Ruth Wallace identified four conventional beliefs about gender that underlie sexism in the workplace. First is the belief that there are natural differences between the two sexes—men are bigger, stronger, and more objective; women are more loving, nurturing, and emotional—that make some work more appropriate for men and other work more appropriate for women. Second is the belief that men should be in authority and that authority carries with it certain obligations about earning a living and providing for one's family. Third is the belief that the world is divided into public and private spheres and that men's work belongs to the former while women's work belongs to the latter. Fourth is the idea that women's work outside the home is always temporary and will be interrupted as soon as the woman bears a child. Along with this goes the belief that women work because they want to and not because they have to.

Although women have been present in virtually all occupations since the 1950s, this set of beliefs continues to have an impact on how women's work is valued. In the more highly paid professions women have been more successful in taking stands against sex discrimination because they have the financial resources to provide themselves and their families with paid help to care for children and do the housework that is still largely the woman's responsibility.

For the vast majority of American women, however, work outside the home is a financial necessity, and the jobs open to them are low paying. Thirty-five percent of all households headed by women fall below the poverty line. In 32 percent of African-American households, married women work; even with their addition to the family's income, the average yearly income for an African-American family is only $22,795.

Sex discrimination is as pervasive, if not more pervasive, among working-class occupations as it is among the professions. During the 1980s, 75 percent of all girls in vocational education programs in the United States were trained for careers in consumerism, homemaking, and health-allied fields. Seventy-five percent of all boys, on the other hand, were trained for jobs in agriculture, technology, and heavy industry. The jobs available to the boys paid significantly higher wages than those available to the girls.

GENDER-RELATED DIFFERENCES

At the root of the sex bias in employment is the biological fact that women are the only sex who can bear children. This reality is often coupled with the belief that pregnancy and early childhood care are drains on a woman's productivity in the workplace. Along with this, of course, is the sense that the qualities associated with bearing and rearing small children—nurture and care—are more appropriate to work such as nursing and teaching. Whether the position is one of the corporate management jobs susceptible to the "Mommy Track" or work as a part-time nurse's aide (a job that might allow the woman to be home when her children arrive from school), woman's work is perceived to be affected by her potential for having children.

In 1978 Congress passed the Pregnancy Disability Amendment to Title VII of the Civil Rights Act, which outlawed discrimination against pregnant women in all areas of employment and required that employers who offer health insurance and temporary disability plans cover pregnancy and childbirth under such plans. A number of other programs have recently been introduced by farsighted employers who recognize the value of all people, regardless of gender, to the overall productivity and well-being of society. Parental leave, instead of maternity leave, means that either parent may take time off to care for young children. In this way a woman whose career is at a critical point may opt to remain in the workplace and perhaps not lose out on a promotion.

Day care facilities at work are also critical for working parents. Mothers and fathers who can be assured of high-quality care for their children and who can have ready access to their children during the day—in case of illness, routine medical care, or just plain nurturing time—are less likely to miss work. Day care costs are high, and employers must bear some of these costs. However, employee absenteeism also costs the employer, and absenteeism is not an easily controlled cost. With better day care facilities women's absenteeism for child care reasons would inevitably drop.

Nor should pregnancy be viewed as the sole

*As more families require two incomes, the need
for quality day care and preschools increases.*

gender-related difficulty for employers. A recent study showed that alcohol abuse is a major factor in employee absenteeism. Men in the work force are far more likely than women to be alcohol abusers. Forty-three percent of men who drink are moderate-to-heavy alcohol abusers, whereas only 18 percent of women fit this description. It is discriminatory to base business practices on conditions that are characteristic of one sex but ignore the real costs of other gender-linked behavior.

Besides alcohol abuse other predominantly male practices take a heavy toll on businesses. As Audrey Freedman has pointed out, "Another heavy but ignored cost of employing men is their greater inclination to engage in destructive struggles for control. Corporate takeover battles waste billions of dollars in capital and productive energy."[3] For both sexes, discrimination is wrong and wastes both financial and human resources. The male executive whose alcoholism goes untreated because his collegues view him as one of the "good old boys" is harmed as much as the woman who is passed over for promotion because she is thinking of starting a family.

DISCRIMINATION IN THE JUSTICE SYSTEM

Modern sex discrimination is not limited to the workplace. The justice system in the United States—laws, courts, and prisons—is fraught with sexism. Sex discrimination is evident in the definition of crimes involving sexual behavior (especially rape and prostitution), law enforcement practices, the treatment of juvenile delinquents, the treatment of prisoners, and the handling of divorce and custody cases.

The legal system in the United States, like employment practices, bases its treatment of men and women on assumptions about sex roles that are outmoded and complex. Modern courts, for example, have traditionally granted women custody of young children in cases of divorce. For the custodial mother to leave her home for the purposes of education or a paying job has been viewed as grounds for loss of custody. Her role as mother, this argument runs, is weakened by her activities outside the home. Courts awarding custody have had nothing but praise, however, for a father who attends night classes or works longer hours. If the father's role is breadwinner, then his main function should be to work outside the home. These gender categories do not allow for individual variations: the mother who must work from financial necessity or who works at a satisfying job that makes her a happier person and better mother, or the father who accepts a lower-paying job with shorter hours in order to spend more time with his children.

Perhaps no area of the law is more discriminatory than the juvenile code. Sentences for juvenile offenders often are determined by sex. In recent years girls outnumbered boys two to one in facing legal consequences for such crimes as truancy, promiscuity, and incorrigibility. Boys are often expected to skip school, run away from home, experiment sexually, and generally rebel. Consequently, they are less likely to face court action for such behavior. Girls, on the other hand, are expected to behave in a more docile manner. For that reason girls who run away, who engage in early sexual relations, or who skip school are treated more harshly by the courts. Girls may even be incarcerated in reform schools or juvenile detention halls for "crimes" that are excused in boys. In the 1960s and 1970s girls tended to be imprisoned, on average, for longer periods of time than were boys.

Women who have broken the law also find that their treatment differs from that of male prisoners. As late as 1980 only one state had more than a single prison for women because women prisoners made up such a small percentage of the prison population. For structural reasons women prisoners were frequently incarcerated far away from their families and could not participate in visitation programs to the same extent that men could. Women are far less likely than men to be released for work details, and, like vocational education students, women prisoners tend to be trained for lower-paying, lower-status occupations. Although very few women work as prison guards in male prisons, many men hold jobs guarding women prisoners, especially in the higher levels (and higher-paying levels) of prison administration.

On the job and in the eyes of the law, women in American society are not yet equal to men. Nineteenth-century stereotypes about women's and men's roles have yet to catch up with the realities of the workplace and changing family structures in industrial twentieth-century America. The "feminization of poverty," a catch phrase used to describe the increasing percentages of women and dependent children living below the poverty line, is one result of this disjunction between myth and reality. Until all Americans take a stand against sex discrimination, the cost to our productivity in dollars and in lives will remain too high.

==SEVEN==

HOW TO BECOME INVOLVED

In the fight against sex discrimination, people have found many ways to take a stand. Abigail Adams and her contemporaries used letter writing, petitions, and moral suasion to persuade the men in power to share that power with them. The suffragists of the nineteenth and early twentieth centuries used all of these tactics and more. They marched, held conventions, spoke out at public meetings, campaigned for referenda, and formed local networks. After the Nineteenth Amendment was passed, the associations remained. The NAWSA became the League of Women Voters, an organization that used many of the suffragists' techniques to get people to register to vote. During the women's movement of the 1960s and 1970s, new tactics were added: sit-ins and mass demonstrations, the direct election of women to public office, and campaigns for and against male candidates based on their voting records on women's issues. Finally,

WE
WILL
BE
BACK

Paper Rout
Girls

WE WANT
per
Murphy Q
Top Dep

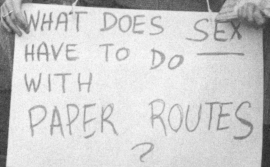

WHAT DOES SEX
HAVE TO DO
WITH
PAPER ROUTES
?

WE DESERVE
EQUAL
TREAT-
MENT!
STARTING
WITH
PAPER ROUTES!!

there were enough women in political offices at both the state and national level of women to form their own political caucuses.

SEXISM IN THE SCHOOLS

As long as sex discrimination continues, all of these ways and more must be used by everyone—people in politics and ordinary citizens—to take a stand. Individuals can fight for their own right to act in areas that may not traditionally encourage participation by members of their sex. For boys and girls, sports is often the arena in which they take a stand. Title IX of the Education Amendment of 1972 states that "no person in the United States shall, on the basis of sex, be excluded from participation, be denied the benefits of, or be subjected to discrimination under any education program or activity receiving federal financial assistance." In many cases this means sports programs. Girls have successfully begun to participate in Little League baseball and on soccer and football teams. For Tad Roemer, a senior in a New York State high school, Title IX has meant a chance for him to play on the varsity field hockey team. For Tad to gain permission to play, he had to appeal to the sectional board overseeing his school's sports program, and he had to agree to wear the traditional field hockey kilt.

In the early seventies, these girls protested discrimination in a particular form of employment: having a paper route.

Other areas of school life can be places to take a stand against sex discrimination. Student council and class officers tend to fall along gender lines. Boys are often elected presidents, and girls are often elected to serve as secretaries. Running for offices not traditionally held by one's sex or supporting candidates who are trying to be the first male secretary or the first female president—providing they are well qualified for the offices they are running for—are ways to take a stand against sexism.

Textbooks can also be a source of sex discrimination. Students as well as teachers can look critically at textbooks. Are all of the authors men? Do pictures and stories present women and men in traditional roles? For example, are all of the boys engaged in interesting activities while girls stand by passively and watch? Is a course on great American authors limited to William Faulkner, Mark Twain, Ralph Waldo Emerson, F. Scott Fitzgerald, Ernest Hemingway, and Nathaniel Hawthorne, with little or no mention of female authors?

This kind of discriminatory reading list should be brought to the attention first of the teacher, then the principal, and finally the board of education. Through letters and petitions students can ensure that the curriculum is gender-balanced.

SEXISM IN THE MEDIA

Television and movies are also sources of sex discrimination because they often show characters who are stereotyped according to sex. Because movies are dependent on consumers for their popularity, people can have great influence over what is produced by Hollywood in the way of entertainment. A survey in 1982 of prime-time television programs showed that strong male characters outnumbered female characters by three to one. In addition, fewer than 20 percent of the women on television were portrayed as working outside the home, whereas in real life the number is well over 50 percent. Viewers can change these misconceptions by boycotting shows that present sexist images and by writing to producers, to networks, and to magazines and newspapers listing or reviewing local television offerings.

GOING TO COURT

Other stands against sex discrimination can be made through the courts. Many women pay higher life insurance premiums or receive lower annuity payments because women, on average, live longer than men. Feminist groups have hired lawyers to fight this discrimination in court. Other groups have successfully overturned the males-only membership policies of private clubs. They have been able to prove in court that those clubs are centers of political and economic power and that their exclusionary membership policies deny women equal access to power.

Sensitivity to language is also very important. Colleges and high schools that refer to their female students as girls or young ladies and their male students as men send a not-so-subtle message about the relative importance of each sex. When a high school posts the schedule for the varsity soccer team and the girls' varsity soccer team, the message is clear. Boys are the real varsity; girls' teams are second class. The federal government, like many other institutions, is guilty of sexist language. In categorizing employment, the Census Bureau divides married-couple families into those with a "wife" in the paid labor force and those without. There is no provision in this kind of accounting for married-couple households where the woman is the chief breadwinner and the man cares for the house and children. Looking for discriminatory language and protesting its usage are ways of taking a stand against sexism.

Sexual harassment is another form of sex discrimination that everyone must fight. The notion that men in superior positions are free to make suggestive propositions to the women with whom they work is unacceptable. Women and other men must protest these actions directly, and employers must be prepared to fire offenders.

EIGHT

SOME PROFILES OF
YOUNG ACTIVISTS

JANE

From the time she was in first grade, Jane Scott
loved to play soccer. Her town had a soccer league
for boys and girls, and Jane played on a team in
that league for five summers. She was not as tall as
some of the other players, but she was strong and
fast. During her last season playing town soccer,
she was co-captain of the team for eleven-and-
younger.

When Jane entered junior high, she found that
boys and girls played on separate teams. Jane
played happily and successfully on the girls' team
during seventh and eighth grades, and she occa-

* The names of the young people profiled in this chapter have been
changed.

125

sionally had the opportunity to watch the high school girls' varsity play. She could not wait to be a member of the varsity.

During her first few days of high school, Jane tried out for varsity soccer. To her great joy, she found that she was the only freshman to make the team. Although she sat on the bench for most of her first season, Jane was told by the coach that she had great potential and would be a key player as she got older.

What the coach promised came true in Jane's sophomore year. She started in every game and occasionally was high scorer.

After each game Jane eagerly looked through the newspaper for reports on the game. She was always disappointed. On the other hand, the paper regularly published pictures and stories of the boys' games along with scores. Jane looked in vain for any mention of the girls' team, either at her school or any other.

She talked to her coach, who said that he usually phoned in the team's score to the sports desk at the newspaper but had no control over whether or not the score was reported. Nor did he remember ever seeing a reporter or photographer at a girls' game, even though a sportswriter frequently attended the boys' matches. The coach suggested that Jane contact the paper directly. To Jane the paper's coverage of local high school sports seemed to be sex discrimination.

Jane called the sports desk and asked about coverage of girls' teams. The sports editor told her that there was only so much space in a newspaper, and furthermore, no one ever submitted reports about the girls' teams. He told Jane that she was welcome to write an account of the next game, and if it was good enough, the paper would publish the story.

Jane wrote the story, and the paper published it. The next day the sports editor called her and asked if she would like a volunteer job covering all girls' sports in the area. Jane accepted, and the next summer she became a paid member of the newspaper staff. Jane had taken a stand against sex discrimination and had obtained her first job at the same time.

JACK

Jack Shea grew up in an unusual household. His father was a chef at a large resort, so Jack lived in an apartment on the grounds of the resort. Jack was allowed to roam freely throughout the grounds. He swam in the pool, learned to play tennis and golf, and helped out in the stables. With all of the resort to choose from, Jack's favorite place was the kitchen, where his father worked. He liked to help the baker and was soon skilled at decorating cakes.

When Jack's older sister entered junior high, she enrolled in a home economics class, where she began to learn formally about cooking. Jack was excited about the possibility of enrolling in a similar class when he entered seventh grade.

Jack met with his guidance counselor the week before he entered junior high in order to plan his schedule. When he told the guidance counselor that he wanted to enroll in a cooking class, he was shocked to hear "Boys take shop or mechanical drawing. Only girls are allowed to take cooking."

Jack did not know what to do. When he left the guidance office, Jack ran into two of his friends. He explained what had happened. To his chagrin, they were unsympathetic. One of them shrugged and implied that only "sissies" would want to take cooking.

On his way home Jack ran into his sixth-grade teacher, a woman he admired very much. Glumly, he told her about his problem. She listened and then suggested that Jack write a letter to the principal. He did so.

After the principal received Jack's letter, he called Jack into his office. Although he was friendly, he did not agree with Jack, and he suggested that it would be more "manly" of Jack to take shop or mechanical drawing.

Jack's conversation with the principal made him mad. Furthermore, he had found three other boys who wanted to enroll in the cooking class. Jack decided to pursue the issue further. He asked his English teacher who hired the principal, and she told him that the school board was responsible for hiring administrators.

Jack obtained a list of school board members and sent them a copy of his letter to the principal. The president of the board responded to Jack with an invitation for him and his friends to attend the next board meeting.

With the help of his English teacher, Jack carefully prepared for the meeting. He argued that assigning classes by gender was a form of sex discrimination and was, in fact, illegal according to the law that said schools should offer students equal access to programs, regardless of sex.

The board of education and the lawyers for the board listened respectfully to Jack. They agreed with him. Although it was too late for him to enroll in the cooking class for that semester, he signed up for the spring. At the same time, three girls signed up for mechanical drawing, all thanks to Jack's willingness to take a stand.

TANYA

Tanya Harris dreamed of being the first person in her family to go to college. She worked hard for good grades and scored very well on her first set of SATs. When Tanya met with her guidance counselor, Ms. Arnold, she was shocked to learn how much colleges cost. With the help of her counselor, however, she worked out a budget for herself. Her counselor gave her the names of a number of corporations that offered financial assistance to deserving students. In addition, Tanya decided to look for a summer job in order to begin saving money for college.

Tanya knew that she would not be able to drive to work, so the job had to be within walking distance of her house. Some of her friends had good jobs at malls in the suburbs, but there was no way that Tanya could find transportation to those stores.

Only two blocks from Tanya's house was a grocery store with a sign in the window that said: "Help Wanted. $4.50 to $7.50 starting salary." Tanya went to the manager's office in the store and picked up an application form. When she had filled it in, she took it to the office and asked about the differences in the pay scale. She was told that "checkout girls" started at $4.50 an hour but "stock boys" started at $7.50. Tanya asked if she could be considered for a stock boy position. The manager laughed and said, "Girls are too weak for the job." Tanya, who was on her school's basketball and lacrosse teams, asked him to let her try. He said no. Because she did not want to jeopardize her chance for any job, Tanya stopped arguing.

The next day at school Tanya told Ms. Arnold what had happened. The guidance counselor explained that it was illegal for the store to limit jobs on the basis of gender. She gave Tanya the number of the state labor board. Tanya called and spoke to a representative, who asked her to come in and explain her situation in person. Tanya did, and she found the labor counselor, Mr. Hernandez, most helpful. He told Tanya to apply formally for the job as stock boy and then to return to him if her application was rejected.

Tanya dropped off her application and waited. After a week with no response, she returned to the store. The manager told her he would not hire her. Tanya went back to Mr. Hernandez's office. He arranged to go with her to the grocery store to discuss her application. When the store manager learned who Mr. Hernandez was, he reluctantly agreed to

Even in the age of television, people at the grass roots can effect change.

give Tanya the job, but he warned that she would have to do just as much as the boys with whom she would be working. Tanya happily agreed.

Tanya found that she had no trouble keeping up with the other stock boys. At the end of two months, the store manager commended her for her work and admitted that he had been wrong. By taking a stand against sex discrimination, Tanya was able to earn almost twice as much money for college.

In spite of the strides made in combating sex discrimination in American life, nearly 40 percent of all people polled in a recent newspaper survey said they believed that "all things considered, there are more advantages in being a man in America today." Until sexism is eradicated from institutions and, most important, from the myths about women's and men's natural roles that underpin American culture, human beings will be limited by their gender.

The fight to liberate this nation from sexism began in colonial times. People of all ages have been and continue to be engaged in these battles. The success of these battles can be measured in the new definitions of men's and women's work and roles that have transformed late-twentieth-century American society.

A PARTIAL DIRECTORY OF
WOMEN RIGHT'S ORGANIZATIONS

PRIVATE ORGANIZATIONS

National Coalition against Domestic Violence
P.O. Box 15127
Washington, D.C. 20003

National Organization for Women
1401 New York Ave. N.W.
Washington, D.C. 20005

National Women's Law Center
1010 P Street N.W.
Washington, D.C. 20036

Wider Opportunities for Women
1325 G Street N.W.
Washington, D.C. 20005

Women's Equity Action League
1250 Eye Street N.W.
Washington, D.C. 20005

GOVERNMENT AGENCIES

Justice Department
Civil Rights Division
Main Justice Building
Washington, D.C. 20530

Labor Department
Women's Bureau
200 Constitution Ave. N.W.
Washington, D.C. 20210

SOURCE NOTES

CHAPTER 1

1. "Poll Finds Women's Gains Have Been Taking a Toll," *New York Times,* August 21, 1989, p. 14.

CHAPTER 2

1. E. H. Clarke, *Sex in Education, or A Fair Chance for Girls* (Boston: J. R. Osgood, 1873), pp. 156–57.
2. Marie-Louise Janssen-Jurreit, *Sexism: The Male Monopoly on History and Thought* (New York: Farrar, Straus, & Giroux, 1982), p. 4.
3. Sara Bennett Stein, *Girls and Boys: The Limits of Nonsexist Child-Rearing* (New York. Scribner's, 1983), p. 173.
4. Janssen-Jurreit, p. 156.
5. Ibid., p. 223.
6. Quoted in Carol Hymowitz and Michaele Weissman, *A History of Women in America* (New York: Bantam Books, 1978), p. 4.

CHAPTER 3

1. Quoted in Hymowitz and Weissman, pp. 26–27.
2. Ibid., p. 26.

3. Ibid., p. 36.
4. Ibid.
5. Quoted in Sara M. Evans, *Born for Liberty* (New York, Macmillan, 1989), p. 58.
6. Ibid., p. 54.
7. Ibid., p. 63.
8. Quoted in Hymowitz and Weissman, p. 81.
9. Ibid.
10. Ibid.
11. Ibid., p. 82.

CHAPTER 4

1. Quoted in Hymowitz and Weissman, p. 82.
2. Ibid., p. 115.
3. Ibid., p. 158.

CHAPTER 5

1. Quoted in Evans, p. 153.
2. Quoted in Hymowitz and Weissman, p. 278.
3. Quoted in Evans, p. 201.
4. Barbara A. Brown et al., *Women's Rights and the Law* (New York: Praeger Press, 1977), p. 2.

CHAPTER 6

1. Quoted in Bruce Leone and M. Teresa O'Neil, *Male/Female Roles: Opposing Viewpoints* (St. Paul, MN: Greenhaven Press, 1983), p. 17.
2. Karen DeCrow, *The Young Woman's Guide to Liberation* (Indianapolis, IN: Pegasus, 1971).
3. Audrey Freedman, "Those Costly Good Old Boys," *New York Times,* July 12, 1989.

FOR FURTHER READING

Birke, Lynda. *Women, Feminism and Biology: The Feminist Challenge.* New York: Methuen, 1986.

Brown, Barbara A., Ann E. Freedman, Harriet N. Katz, and Alice M. Price. *Women's Rights and the Law.* New York: Praeger Press, 1977.

Ehrenreich, B., and D. English. *For Her Own Good.* New York: Doubleday, 1989.

Eisenstein, Sarah. *Give Us Bread but Give Us Roses.* London: Routledge and Kegan Paul, 1983.

Evans, Sara M. *Born for Liberty: A History of Women in America.* New York: Macmillan, 1989.

Glazer, Perina M., and Miriam Slater. *Unequal Colleagues: The Entrance of Women into the Professions, 1890–1940.* New Brunswick, NJ: Rutgers University Press, 1987.

Gluck, Sherna B. *Rosie the Riveter Revisited: Women, the War and Social Change.* Boston: Twayne Publishers, 1987.

Hymowitz, Carol, and Michaele Weissman. *A History of Women in America.* New York: Bantam Books, 1978.

Lengermann, Patricia M., and Ruth A. Wallace. *Gender in America.* Englewood Cliffs, NJ: Prentice-Hall, 1985.

Scott, Hilda. *Working Your Way to the Bottom: The Feminization of Poverty.* London: Pandora, 1984.

Stein, Sara Bennett. *Girls and Boys: The Limits of Nonsexist Child-Rearing*. New York: Scribner's, 1983.

Weiner, Lynn W. *From Working Girl to Working Mother: The Female Labor Force in the United States, 1820–1980*. Chapel Hill, NC: University of North Carolina Press, 1985.

INDEX

ABOUT
THE AUTHOR

Trudy J. Hanmer is acting principal of the Emma Willard School in Troy, New York. She holds a master's degree in American history from the University of Virginia.

Ms. Hanmer is the author of a number of other books for Franklin Watts, including *Uganda, Haiti, The Growth of Cities,* and *The Advancing Frontier.* She lives in Troy, New York.